T0356306

LETTERS TO MARTIN

MEDITATIONS ON DEMOCRACY IN BLACK AMERICA

RANDAL MAURICE JELKS

Lawrence Hill Books

Chicago

Copyright © 2022 by Randal Maurice Jelks
All rights reserved
Published by Lawrence Hill Books
An imprint of Chicago Review Press Incorporated
814 North Franklin Street
Chicago, Illinois 60610
ISBN 978-1-64160-603-5

Library of Congress Control Number: 2021946428

Typesetting: Nord Compo

Printed in the United States of America
5 4 3 2 1

To

Lerone Bennett Jr.
(October 28, 1928–February 14, 2018)
Your *Ebony* magazine features instructed me
in the artful lyricism of a people's history.

Jess Gill
(February 24, 1932–April 4, 2001)
My uncle, "I love you more today than yesterday."
You stood alongside Martin and fathered me
when I needed it most.

Dr. Darlene Clark Hine
My PhD mentor who insisted that Black women's histories
reconfigured US history itself.

Edward Nelson III
(March 16, 1928–June 13, 1989)
My beloved Uncle June, the first man in my life,
you taught me quiet determination and dignity to overcome.
Every morning I wake up I am reminded
to imitate your courage.

CONTENTS

PROLOGUE

The Constitution
A noble piece of paper
With free society
Struggled but it died in vain
—Gil Scott-Heron, "Winter in America"[1]

Martin,

In late 2016, I was invited to Elmhurst College, the alma mater of two great theologians, brothers H. Richard and Reinhold Niebuhr. Their legacies in academia and in public life still resonate. They were, of course, titans in your student years at Crozer Seminary and Boston University. Their books were required reading. As your fame rose, you would have occasion to converse and correspond with the both of them. So I was deeply honored to be invited to this small college that shaped these two vitally important theologians who influenced your thought.

It was a propitious moment. The country had been shocked by the presidential election of 2016. Like the presidential election of 2000, the forces of conservatism that began with the election of Ronald Reagan in 1980 still vice-gripped political power. The election of Donald J. Trump was the apotheosis of

Reagan-era conservatism. Both Reagan and Trump were masters of television, and they both used it to reward the superrich. While Ronald Reagan won his election with the legitimacy of an overwhelming majority of the American voters, Trump lost the popular vote by two million but won the electoral college, assuring him the presidency. His presidency, like that of former president George W. Bush in 2000, had an air of illegitimacy. In 2000, the Supreme Court awarded the election to Bush over his opponent Al Gore, instead of ordering Florida to have an extensive recount. It left the nation in a tizzy. The Bush administration used the court's decree to nearly ruin the country in an inadvisable war, worse than Vietnam. Bush forty-three's global aggression and domestic flubs were so reckless they opened up the lane for Barack Obama to be elected as the country's first African American president.

The Obama administration was deliberate and overall above reproach when it came to scandals within his administration. His presidency was "No drama Obama!" The problem for President Obama was that he was unwilling to be Machiavellian against his GOP opponents at the start of his administration. He thought being a Black patrician necessitated honorable politics. Though Obama was an outstanding steward of the office, his politics did not make his opponents, or his allies, fear him. Further, he allowed the Tea Party to fester. The Tea Party was funded by some of the country's wealthiest families, who were looking to end the limited social safety net of Franklin Roosevelt's New Deal and its expansion under Lyndon Johnson's Great Society program. This was a long-term strategy that of course required dominating the federal courts with conservative appointees. These moguls of finance, media, and technology, using Orwellian doublespeak, pushed monopoly as free enterprise. Obama responded carefully and responsibly, but not aggressively. His

noblesse-oblige style of politics did not serve his rainbow coalition or hold them together after he left office.

Obama supported his former secretary of state, Hillary Clinton,
who by all measures was more qualified than any of her male
counterparts. The problem for Clinton was her political tin ear
and her past politics tied to her husband's moderate conservatism. In 1992 Bill Clinton ran as a Walmart Democrat, a southern
politician who recognized that, to get elected, he had to accept
a low-wage service economy. He won, but his policies tended to
favor corporate and financial sectors over labor. He was friendly,
but at a distance, with organized labor. In addition, fearing his
GOP opponents, he signed into law the Personal Responsibility
and Work Opportunity Reconciliation Act. This draconian crime
bill put the onus on women alone to take care of their children,
with limited support from the state in terms of public education
and access to childcare. This bill was baked with sexist flour and
decorated with racist icing and welfare-queen figurines. It was a
bootstraps approach to the economic deindustrialization that had
begun tearing through all sectors of working-class America in the
late 1970s. Construed with racist and sexist bias, the bill harmed
the Black communities who overwhelmingly voted for Clinton.

Hillary Clinton was the bearer of her husband's legacy, and she
had no good defense of his or her former actions in the wake of
Michael Brown Jr.'s murder by police in Ferguson, Missouri. They
had asked Black voters to vote for them, but their policy actions
did the greatest harm to a community that was the most loyal to
the Democratic Party. Black people, both as a racial group and as
working-class constituents, lost with the policy conservatism of
the Democratic Leadership Council. Hillary Clinton's campaign
stumbled in 2008 against Obama, and once more it stumbled
in 2016. She was unable to address her own past policy deci-
sions robustly, especially when it came to race and class status. In

addition, conservative propaganda spewed enough misogynistic tales that blurred who she really was as a candidate. Though Clinton won the popular vote by two million, she lost the electoral college to Trump. She failed to speak to the woes of the working classes and lost the Great Lakes states. Her loss was crushing.

I was invited to Elmhurst College a few weeks after President Trump's inauguration to office. In the quarters I keep it was a dispiriting time. So I wanted to say something hopeful to the young people that I would address. I wanted them to know that democracy in the United States has always been difficult to secure. It is a constant fight. Like Reinhold Niebuhr I believe democracies are not always assured. He knew this from witnessing the rise of Nazism in Germany and a totalitarian form of communism in the Soviet Union. Niebuhr was right to be theologically pessimistic. Human self-aggrandizement throughout recorded history is a constant reality. It is a reality being witnessed today in every outsized leader who manages to control state power and enshrine themselves monarchically. However, different from Niebuhr, I recognize that hope and struggle are central to our sojourn as a people. Our collective sojourn demands that we think about ways to create a better democracy. Our forebearers stubbornly held onto the idea that freedom of the self and self-governance are sacred realities. They are to be cherished. They are sacred because our freedoms have always been tenuous and always in jeopardy. This has been central to our spiritual histories.

So the day I arrived at Elmhurst I wanted to acknowledge Reinhold Niebuhr's clear-eyed pessimism but also center the hope that you embodied. In my mind, you personified many of the central spiritual themes of Black histories. In your sermonic mobilizations, you called us to resist an all-encompassing, dehumanizing political apartheid. As you learned from your mentors, this struggle was to overcome disfigurement of the self, as well as a disfigured society.[2] This struggle was always as much spiritual as it was material.

I arrived at Elmhurst on what was, for February in the Chicago area, a wonderful, partially sunny day. I came with a buoyant and open spirit, hoping to uplift students gripped by fears. What I wanted them to know was that spirituality, however they defined it, is as much a part of building, maintaining, and spreading democracy as anything else in their lives. Thus came the idea of these meditations.

I thought what I could offer these students were my thoughts on how to use their spirituality to engage in democratic struggles. I wanted them to know that the struggle to live democratically is lifelong. It is a never-ending battle on multiple fronts. But also, my intention was then, as here, to critically inspire and reassess the meaningfulness of democratic struggle by giving reflection on your words. In my mind their spirits needed bolstering in the face of this overwhelming labor, and I wanted the young people at Elmhurst College to hear a message of solidarity and hope. The greatest lesson the civil rights movement teaches us is how to face our fears and push back against powerful collective self-interests, even in the face of death. As I prepared for the talk, I kept listening to Sweet Honey in the Rock's "Ella's Song." The goal of my talk came to me in this stanza:

> Struggling myself don't mean a whole lot, I've come to realize
> That teaching others to stand up and fight is the only way my struggle survives.[3]

I wanted to ignite the students' spiritual imaginations and for their spirits to not be dampened. I wanted them to know that we could face our difficult days together. I decided to offer them a meditation, not solely analysis—like the Apostle Paul and the epistle form that you, Martin, used so beautifully in Birmingham to answer your critics regarding the Southern Christian Leadership Conference's (SCLC) organized protest. So it was my desire to define democratic struggle through an inward journey.

These pages, too, are an exigent spiritual appeal. Democracy is more than consumerist choices that are so easily manipulated and algorithmically controlled. The heart of democracy is the internalization of genuine equality and respect for others, no matter their persuasions or incomes. This respect must be at the core of our being. Democracy is about the recognition that limitations must be placed upon absolute power—the power to enslave, the power to politically dominate, the power to make destructive warfare and murderous genocides. This is the essence of our fight in rebuilding our society's foundations. Our difficult days call for us to summon democracy's winds and fill our lungs with fresh air. In the words of your longtime Christian spiritual mentor, Howard Thurman:

> The movement of the Spirit of God in the hearts of men and women often calls them to act against the spirit of their times or causes them to anticipate a spirit which is yet in the making. In a moment of dedication they are given wisdom and courage to dare a deed that challenges and to kindle a hope that inspires.[4]

1

NETWORK OF MUTUALITY

Wake up, everybody
No more sleepin' in bed
No more backward thinkin'
Time for thinkin' ahead
—Harold Melvin & the Blue Notes,
"Wake Up Everybody"[1]

Martin,

I read that some of your closest peers called you Martin, and others called you Mike. I thought of you as Martin after seeing your photograph in John Williams's book *The King That God Didn't Save* when I was thirteen. There was only you and Andrew Young in the Birmingham airport, around 4:00 AM. You were slumped over with a cigarette in your hand, exhausted. You were weary like the men who labored in my childhood neighborhood of New Orleans, drooped over after a week's worth of physical toil from jobs that paid too little money. They were, like you, trying to preserve enough energy to enjoy families and friends. They, too, slumped over in barrooms and on their front porches with

7

a cigarette and a beer, fatigued. That photograph reminded me of southern Black and White men known only by their initials, not their full names. To me, you were not Mike, your former birth name and nickname. That name bore a childhood familiarity I dared not broach. In my eyes you were Martin in the same way they were the E.J.s and A.B.s throughout the South. At thirteen years of age, that photograph offered me a lesson in your humanity. You were not the icon of *Ebony* magazine. You were an exhausted worker. That photograph was not the Reverend Dr. Martin Luther King Jr., it was Martin the overworked laborer. The toil of your labor had taken it out of you.

As exhausted as you appeared to be in that photo, there was still something beautiful about it. You were James Brown short. You looked like the dark-skinned men in my communities whom I saw at the barbershop, in church, and on the street corners—you held the same Black handsomeness that US society so fears. This is something men in our community loved about you secretly, even if they disagreed with you on questions of self-defense. You were dark as they were, short, with a wide Black African nose, and you had hair that you brushed to smooth out the naps.

Further, you shared Black hilarity. Behind closed doors you exhibited stylistically the irreverent ribald humor that I heard from men on my streets and from my uncles.[2] You were filled with off-color remarks, wisecracks on topics from politics to sex. Though you looked dog-tired, I wondered what you told Andrew Young as the two of you waited for the airplane back to Atlanta. I am certain that, even in your weariness, there was a funny exchange. The blues is serious merriment. As I look back on that captured moment now, I am sure you and Young had a laughable signifying moment about the dire situations the movement faced. You had to laugh to keep from crying. The fact is that your constant toiling on the road took you away from home too much. You spent nearly all your adult life on the road, organizing to build a truly democratic society. This was your zeitgeist, the spirit of the time.

And here we are once more with the spirit of the time moving folks out to march in the streets, this time fraught with a deadly global virus. They are righteously outraged that democracy, the participatory self-governance that was supposed to have been created to deliver justice for all, is slipping the public's grasp. They fear the United States has become unexceptional. The election of President Trump evoked mass protestations from Black men and women, women generally, and scientists. These marches have had one aim: moving to build a more inclusive democracy, one where economic and social inclusion meet to build a more participatory and just society.

It has been over fifty years since your death, and as you prophesized shortly before your death, our struggles have been difficult. The optimistic dream you exhorted before the Lincoln Memorial in hindsight sometimes seems Kafkaesque.[3] Your dream was a burdensome responsibility. You realized that it was more systemic than personal and made up of more structural considerations than individual impressions. And today the battles in our streets are even more explicitly about the corporate economic disparities and militarized police departments who enforce a rule of law to protect power, not people. Martin, you would be surprised to know there are still too many Bull Connors on our streets who carry out their brutality with the blessings of governors, judges, mayors, and robber barons. All attempt to corral our resistances using intimidation and force, as though our humanity does not count. However, as you knew, and I know too, our lives have always mattered. This has been the religious doctrine instilled in us. We are all God's children. This has been our great spiritual equalizer, and it has followed us in our histories. It is profoundly democratic.

You were of my parents' generation. It would have been impossible for me to have called you by your first name in your lifetime. I was a child, and you were an adult. I was born ten months after the Montgomery bus boycott began. I was witness, participant, and beneficiary of the unfolding drama called the civil rights movement. Strange as it may seem, as a youngster, I felt an intimacy with you as I do today—call it our network of mutuality. This mutuality for me came in my adolescence.

I think of you now because the consensus is that the United States as the greatest moral country in the world has come to an end. That idea was promoted by a corporate elite who touted a God-fearing America, though they behaved godlessly in defense of capitalism. They promoted the idea that the United States' God-fearing citizens lived in opposition to the godless Soviet Union.[4] They preached private property and felt menaced by the likes of Cuba's Fidel Castro. Now there were and still are real political differences at stake regarding governing philosophies. But no matter the government, aggrandizement of power is perennially an original sin. In the United States, the stain of the forbidden fruit has been racism. Black men's and women's visibility constantly reminded the country of its inglorious fiction—that all people have equal advantages to "life, liberty, and the pursuit of happiness." The Blackness of the United States, let alone throughout the Americas, serves as counternarrative to fictive notions of Jeffersonian democracy.

In our country the histories of Black people were intentionally hidden. Even today American history is mashed up like white potatoes without the brown gravy, belying the nation's Eurocentrism. Truth is, Black people have been the most democratic because we had to be. We were constantly resisting our degraded plights. Black laborers, from store clerks to fast-food servers, constantly organized against exploitation from enslavement, sharecropping, meatpacking, and auto-making. Black women laborers relentlessly ruptured the gendered social order, stonewalling long before there was a riot in New York City. Black histories shred the mythologies of the American Revolution, Lincoln freeing the slaves, Lost Causes, and landings on Plymouth Rock. Our histories are contrapuntal. They defy the idea that people of the United States are God-fearing. If anything, it is our histories that are exceptional. We have been the ones that have demonstrated a commitment to being democratic.[5]

I began learning these lessons early. In 1960, Ruby Bridges, a six-year-old, only two years my senior, was escorted by US marshals to William Frantz School in downtown New Orleans. That scene was made famous by Norman Rockwell's painting. Hazily I recollect the whispered tones of adult discussion in our narrow shotgun house about federal officers escorting a child near my age to school. My mother, uncle, and grandmother must have held similar discussions as soldiers escorted teenagers to Little Rock High School. It is nearly unforgivable the vitriol that came from the lips of White mothers as they chanted from Little Rock to New Orleans: "Two, four, six, eight, we don't want to niggergrate!" And nothing brought it home like September 15, 1963, seven days before my seventh birthday—the bombing of the Sixteenth Street Baptist Church that killed four girls attending Sunday School. They were my generational peers.

And the struggle continued through my pubescence. The Audubon Park swimming pool was the largest in Uptown New Orleans. It was shut down in 1961, ostensibly because of expensive repairs. In truth it was to prevent multihued children from joining White ones for a swim. The pool did not reopen until I was twelve, in 1969. My *Wonder Years*, as the nostalgic, baby-boomer television show was titled, were filled with protest and Mardi Gras festivities. Protests took place all around me. Those protestations seeped into our front stoops, playground banter, and comic book arguments—whether Kato of *The Green Hornet* got his rightful due as a colored man. Those years were inflected by rightful rage. And everywhere, Black children and youth were at the center. From the 1930s onward, Black youth were what V. I. Lenin called the revolutionary vanguard. They were in a fight to advance democracy. And this was before the Black Panther Party became strapped. Martin, my wonder years were also shaped by your preachments.

It was your assassination that awakened me to the revolution. Your death that early evening in April helped me to connect dots about our prevailing social order. To this day I have kept wrapped in mylar the New Orleans *Times-Picayune* with its headline of your assassination. I was eleven.

The Monday after your murder, we returned to school. My sixth-grade teacher, Mr. Price, put me in charge of running the phonograph the entire day, playing your sermons and speeches. Our class sat quietly and listened to your sermons that had been recorded by Motown Records. "I Have a Dream," "A Knock at Midnight," and "Drum Major Instinct." And in between listening to you, Mr. Price, filled with grief, told our class that we needed to know "our people's history, our struggle!" And this was reinforced when my local YMCA, the "Colored Y," "the Black Y," the Dryades Street YMCA, organized a trip for us to travel to your gravesite on the first anniversary of your death. A hundred or so boys sold candy throughout the city to make this pilgrimage. Our leader, Mr. Arthur Hughes, thought, rightfully in retrospect, that our exposure as adolescent boys would make us more civically engaged. In my case, he was right. That trip was formative. It was the beginning of our relationship. I remember your sermon "Remaining Woke Through a Great Revolution"—young people now tell one another to "stay woke!" without knowing where to attribute it. Your words, nevertheless, reverberate.

Through our scientific and technological genius, we have made of this world a neighborhood and yet we have not had the ethical commitment to make of it a brotherhood. But somehow, and in some way, we have got to do this. We must all learn to live together as brothers or we will all perish together as fools. We are tied together in the single garment of destiny, caught in an inescapable network of mutuality. And whatever affects one directly affects all indirectly. For some strange reason I can never be what I ought to be until you are what you ought to be. And you can never be what you ought to be until I am what I ought to be. This is the way God's universe is made; this is the way it is structured.[6]

You were right! Globally, we are tied up in a network of mutuality, though it does not prevent warfare and global jousting for dominance. Personally, we are tied together, though we compete jealously with one another as though we are not. Ecologically, we are tied together, though our polluting behaviors demonstrate our habitual carelessness.

The zeitgeist of democratic struggle continued, and the movement after your death demanded that Black people redefine what it meant to be democratic. We did not have the luxury of being nonquestioning citizens. We were daughters and sons of grand democratic histories. And this required us to think more expansively about what democracy means for ourselves and the nation.

In our mutual southern upbringings, Protestant Christian faith was integral to our democratic politics. These politics were first practiced at our churches; you as a Baptist, and me as a Lutheran. I was reared, educated, and confirmed in the Missouri Synod Lutheran Church. In my earliest school days, I was initially confused between early modern Luther and you. We NOLA Black Lutherans were descendants of late nineteenth-century mission efforts, and we were also the denomination's stepchildren. Though we tried to conform to German American rectitude, our Africanity and Mardi Gras spirit always seemed to interfere. We gyrated below the waist and danced too close. We did not embody the same angst that was expected of our White counterparts—the Augsburg Confessing ones—the heritage that drove Friedrich Nietzsche mad. We took Luther's dictum "Sin, sin boldly! That grace might abound" too literally! Nevertheless, you, like your namesake, spoke your truth as a matter of conscience. It is attributed that Luther said, "Here I stand, I can do no other."[7] Whether he used those words is dubious, but what is truthful is he opposed the closed institutional logic of the Roman Catholic Church that exploited Germanic-speaking peoples. It was Luther's unwavering commitment of his conscience that made your father change his and your names to Martin Luther. Freedom of conscience has always been one of Protestantism's most democratic ethoses.

In 1970, my mother and I moved to Chicago. I loved talking with my uncle about the movement there. He had met you, volunteered as a professional with your efforts, and traveled to Atlanta to hear you preach. He told me about one of your lawyers, Chauncey Eskridge, who also defended Muhammad Ali. I was so enthralled that on a day off from school I went to Eskridge's office to meet him unannounced. Mr. Eskridge's secretary was gracious and quite surprised that a fourteen-year-old wanted to meet a famous Black lawyer. I waited patiently and then was called to see him. I was direct in my inquiry. How was it to defend Dr. King? He patiently answered my questions. In retrospect, those were heady days of Black pride in Chicago. The *Ebony/Jet* building had just opened on Michigan Avenue, radio personality Don Cornelius initially aired a local dance and music television show called *Soul Train*, and Rev. Jesse Jackson Sr., one of your lieutenants, made claims to being the next voice of the movement from his organization PUSH (then named People United to Save Humanity).

I followed your story throughout college. One of the first books I read my freshman year, in between rounds of the card game bid whist, was your *Strength to Love*. I was curious, as I began to think about history as a major, why students—and teachers—didn't understand your intellectual thought in the same way as that of Walt Whitman, William James, and Jonathan Edwards. In my day, only a few of my professors had read W. E. B. Du Bois's *The Souls of Black Folk* or Frederick Douglass's *Narrative of the Life of an American Slave*. It was as though there was no original thought among Black Americans.

This made me eager to engage one of my professors, Harold Cruse, at the University of Michigan. In 1967 Cruse's provocative screed, *The Crisis of the Negro Intellectual*, was published—the year before you were assassinated. That book took Black intellectuals by storm. It was the first time I saw the terms *Negro* and *intellectual* together in a book. In his seminar on civil rights history, I decided to write a paper on your intellectual trajectory. As I researched you, I discovered that many of your biographers focused on the White intellectuals you had read while at Boston University and Crozer Theological Seminary, ignoring the Black authors you had studied while attending Morehouse College. When I wrote my paper for Cruse, I thought I would never come back to you as a subject. That was fictitious. Cruse, in his raspy Virginia-to-Harlem accent, announced to our class, "Mr. Jelks is going to take up the subject of Negro preachers." His statement was prescient. I would also follow your lead in vocational choices—seminary, PhD, and book writing—so I owe a debt to you.

Over fifty years after your death, the fate of US democracy has grown more acute. Our country and the world have spiraled out of control with vainglorious strongmen at the helm, which is why our present situation calls for meditation. It is now time for a spiritual consideration of democracy. By *spiritual* I do not mean "incorporeality." The etymological root of *spiritual* is "air," "breath," or "wind." Breath sustains our living. This is why Eric Garner, the man we witnessed being strangled in a chokehold by the New York police in 2014, breathlessly uttered as he died, "I can't breathe." This is why George Floyd, and so many others, die of abominable strangulations by law enforcement.[8] So my usage of *spiritual* is about the tangible air we breathe, the chemical reality of oxygen that gives us life. In my estimation this is what democracy is all about: the breath of self-respect and respect for others. This is the truth of all great faiths—and democracy is a faith, a belief system. This is why we must consider democracy as a matter of the spirit. Just what does it mean to participate in the governing of ourselves? How does it enhance our daily well-being? How does it inform our personal identities? How does it animate our ethical narratives of power and dominance? These are questions of our spirits.

Your waking hours were spent in the details of a movement. Your work hardly left you time to give careful consideration to the various chords of democracy, though you wrote books on the topic.[9] Your books attempted to spiritually inform mobilization and direct action. They were used to fundraise for the movement. Your fullest statement on democratic protest was your "Letter from Birmingham Jail," in which you articulated why political struggle is a necessary component to a meaningful democracy. That letter continues to inspire and produce air for the dispossessed the world over.

This is why I have culled your words for our present circumstances. Many of us around the globe are unable to breathe. We are now in an era where politics is based on monopolization of resources, driven by gluttonous magnates, politicians who envision themselves to be emperors, and technocrats who enslave us. This is the fuel behind the political economy that is burning down our earth. Our current zeitgeist calls for meditation amid our actions. Reflecting on your words is a starting point, not an end. These meditations are an attempt to go beyond echo chambers. This is especially important as we globally face waves of authoritarian political regimes and an ecosystem precipitously in decline.

This is why I have chosen to write meditations. They are epistolary, similar to the way you wrote your reflections in "Letter from Birmingham Jail". Like the Apostle Paul's letters, which were read to the cosmopolitan congregants from the cities of Corinth, Ephesus, and Rome, these are meant to weave us together and create community. These meditations are resistant to the declension narrative of our political state—made popular by Edward Gibbon's eighteenth-century *The History of the Decline and Fall of the Roman Empire*, and frequently intoned today by historians and journalists.[10] Pundits are right to be fearful about the state of a crumbling US empire; there are real global threats when hegemonic shifts occur. International political threats loom large domestically and abroad. However, it is paralyzing to remain in fear. It requires courage to change circumstances, as the spiritual attests:

> Ain't gonna let nobody turn me around
> Turn me around. . . .
> Keep on a-talkin',
> Marchin' into freedom land.

Courage is at the heart of our linked historical sojourns. It has powered our incessant drive to expand democratic freedoms. European and Anglo-American philosophers in the eighteenth and nineteenth centuries thought at length about self-governance, but that was done primarily by and for an entitled ilk,[11] and democracy for a portion of the population is not in fact democracy. Black folks' history in the United States began with the fight against the multidimensions of enslavement: exploitation of labor, physical confinement, self-loathing, and sexuality. This is why, perhaps, our forebearers best understood the need for self-autonomy, self-rule, and self-determination.[12] This is why our Protestant religious institutions, the ones built by Black hands, emphasized freedom of the self. Here was and is our stone of hope.

To meditate means to slow things down. We need to find perspective even in restive times. Our times are uncertain, perhaps as uncertain as yours. This is why we need reflection. We need to slow down our responses and elongate our breath. Historically, meditations are meant to be regenerative. They are meant to bridge turbulent waters. To that end, these words are meant to be politically encouraging so that we can negotiate our way to a peaceable society.

Martin, you and I have lived entwined in a common zeitgeist of seeking justice. We are tied together historically from one generation to the next by being participants in democratic struggle. Like you, I recognize the necessity for our politics to be guided by something larger than Ayn Rand–style selfishness. There is something more meaningful than that.

> Somewhere we must come to see that human progress never rolls in on the wheels of inevitability. It comes through the tireless efforts and the persistent work of dedicated individuals who are willing to be co-workers with God. And without this hard work, time itself becomes an ally of the primitive forces of social stagnation. So we must help time and realize that the time is always ripe to do right.[13]

2

THE HIGHEST ETHICAL IDEAL

Oh, freedom, oh, freedom, oh, freedom over me
And before I'd be a slave, I'll be buried in my grave
And go home to my Lord and be free
—SUNG BY ODETTA, "OH, FREEDOM!"[1]

Martin,

Being democratic was your highest ethical goal. You felt it was your religious duty and personal obligation. You were a Baptist, and so much of your denominational history was about behaving democratically, even when some pastors were undemocratic in their actions. You knew that Black people understood the concept as though it were inscribed in their national DNA. Black struggle synergized with dissenting English Protestant—Baptist, Presbyterian, Congregationalist—assertion of theological freedoms. It was the freedom of the conscience: the right to object and the right to freely govern oneself. Your voice, rumbling with the timbre of the Deep South blues, thunderously urged us to live up to the noblest aspects of democracy. You reminded us to live ecumenical lives respectfully open to one another. We were to live like this not simply because of the rule of law but also because our lives are inter-linked. In 1963, isolated in the Birmingham city jail, you penned:

> Whatever affects one directly, affects all indirectly. Never again can we afford to live with the narrow, provincial "outside agitator" idea. Anyone who lives inside the United States can never be considered an outsider anywhere within its bounds.[2]

Your steadfast jeremiads urged us to think about our deepest commonalities. From the steps of the Alabama State Capitol you bellowed:

> We must come to see that the end we seek is a society at peace with itself, a society that can live with its conscience. And that will be a day not of the white man, not of the black man. That will be the day of man as man.[3]

You called the country to a high ideal: that democracy's aim is to confer dignity on each of us. Democracy should protect our personhood, which was, in your estimation, divinely imbued. More than Jefferson's rights-based formulations, divinity itself made human beings inviolable.

In Baptist circles that you were nurtured in, spiritual renewal is called a revival. Your revivalist preachments were infused with poetry, and your urgent call to us was to dream expansively. It echoed Joel's prophesizing from Acts 2:17:

> I will pour out my spirit on all flesh;
> your sons and your daughters shall prophesy,
> your old men shall dream dreams,
> and your young men shall see visions.

Democracy, however, is utopian realism. Democratic institutions allow us to dream prophetically within limits. Our dreams always have political implications and are always partial. Our dreams are equally conflictual. In 1936, amid the Great Depression, Langston Hughes penned "Let America Be America Again," a greatly bastardized poem; he understood that dreams are selective.[4]

> O, let America be America again—
> The land that never has been yet—

For Hughes democracy was imagined poetics. Poets push us to widen, or sometimes narrow, the boundaries of self and society. Dreams are our projections. They must be politically and publicly negotiated, as you knew too well:

> I say to you today, my friends, though, so even though we face the difficulties of today and tomorrow, I still have a dream. It is a dream deeply rooted in the American dream.[5]

Your ethical dream defied the political cynicism of your time. The politicians of your time grossly followed Otto von Bismarck, modern Germany's first chancellor, and his mantra that "politics is the art of the possible." The conservative Bismarck, whose nickname was the Iron Chancellor, thought that politics was never an exact science, but a strategic art. His artistry was to keep participatory governance at bay. As brilliant as Bismarck was, neither he, nor the monarchy he represented, ever understood what it meant to live as an oppressed people without self-determination. Your poetic envisioning undid their logic.

At age twenty-six you were swept into a worldwide political maelstrom. Here you were, out front in a globally televised boycott—a protest for common decency and the simplest of rights, the right to ride a bus and take any available seat. As a spokesman for a local movement, you called upon Black people of Montgomery to exhibit the highest democratic ethics—tolerance, mutuality, and conciliation. At the Holt Street Baptist Church, you explained to the audience that they were the embodiment of democracy itself:

> There is never a time in our American democracy that we must ever think we're wrong when we protest. We reserve that right. When labor all over this nation came to see that it would be trampled over by capitalistic power, it was nothing wrong with labor getting together and organizing and protesting for its rights. We, the disinherited of this land, we who have been oppressed so long, are tired of going through the long night of captivity. . . . There is another side called justice. And justice is really love in calculation. Justice is love correcting that which revolts against love.[6]

For over a year, Black people in Montgomery cleaved to one another. With valor they demonstrated collectively that they could face economic, political, and terrorist intimidations. Too often we worship militaristic valor, and I mean no disrespect to forgotten soldiers who die unwillingly on battlefields. But in Montgomery there was valor, armed not with guns but with sheer refusal to conform to injustice. Black Montgomery demonstrated to the world the kind of democratic valor we continually need.

Today we nostalgically look back upon the fighters of those times as though they were mythic heroes, but the protesters in that moment were no nobler than we are today. However, we can gleam wisdom from them: staying organized over a lengthy struggle begins with community. Democracy was practiced among the protesters before they protested. The bus boycott that occurred in Montgomery teaches us that democracy is a life discipline first.

———————

In 1929, the year you were born, Southern state governments were completely nontransparent. They were politically calcified as the "solid South."[7] Although the Three-fifths Compromise had been abandoned with the Thirteenth, Fourteenth, and Fifteenth Constitutional Amendments following the Civil War, a nonvoting Black population remained on the census rolls. This ensured Southern congressional representation without input from Blacks as citizens. Alternative viewpoints and voices were shut up and shut down. The one-party South enforced an economic monopoly that impoverished both Blacks and Whites alike. This insolvency was gleefully evoked in an up-tempo Confederate song:

> Oh, I wish I was in the land of cotton.
> Old times there are not forgotten
> Look away! Look away! Look away! Dixie Land.

The civil rights movement in the South broke this monopoly. It paved the way for new multinational corporations to locate in the region.[8] The historical irony is that those human rights and freedoms that activists fought for opened the Southern economy to international conglomerates in a region always known for the harshest degradation of labor and some of the country's worst human rights abuses. The South became the entrée to the mass manufacturing of foreign automobiles and other goods because of the region's lax labor laws that have historically been used to exploit cheap labor.

Today, once more, the country faces an attempt to squash political participation. In 2013 the US Supreme Court invalidated key provisions in the Voting Rights Act of 1965. This opened Pandora's box, allowing national voter suppression. Today politicians from the old states of the Confederacy have joined those from the Great Lakes to the Great Plains to make it more difficult for citizens to vote. White men, from working class to elite, strive to keep a lock on corporate and political power. Willfully naive citizens do not realize it, but the country as a whole has been "Jim Crowed." The dastardly elimination of voters is the trickery of authoritarian rule.

Martin, all your life you saw Southern politicians stage-manage representative government on behalf of a wealthy ruling minority. Their cynicism, however, did not make you lose heart. Democracy requires continuous cultivation of hope, which first must be internally ploughed. We can never be naive about fellow human beings, but neither can we be misanthropic. Our faith must be that our peers have equal standing in their flaws and strengths. This is in part what the great message of the Abrahamic traditions—Christianity, Islam, and Judaism—has bequeathed to the world. Within our universe we are all created alike from the same dust. This was also the moral goal of the social contract theorists of the seventeenth and eighteenth centuries, who wrestled with barbarous cruelties, genocidal massacres, enslavements, and imperial domination as they thought through questions of human equality and how it might be enacted through democratic governance.[9] They believed that reason and rationality might bring peaceable resolution to European state fractiousness. Their theorizing was based not on actualities, but on a projection that participation in one's own governance would end gruesome warfare. This was faith too.

Your Christian faith had circuitous routes and twisted roots. There was the life-or-death travails of the Middle Passage, in addition to the legion of coffles of the enslaved marching across wooded lands, watering the United States' new empire with a different trail of tears. There was also the African encounter with English dissenters—the Baptists—whose water rites of initiation built community and gave new meaning to the walking dead.

Your faith was not found in a "state of nature," like that of those social contract philosophers Thomas Hobbes, John Locke, and Jean-Jacques Rousseau, whose limited wisdom laid the foundation for our democratic institutions in a secular facsimile of the biblical creation narratives. Rather, your faith was based in a metaphysical belief that human beings are accountable to the divine for how we live together. You assumed that we are to behave with humility, act justly, and show mercy to one another. This faith made you a radical democratic abolitionist.

However, your faith was tempered by the knowledge that human capacity is limited. Sin, you thought, meant that human goodness could be grossly twisted, and the slave ship and the cross were your daily reminders. The ten-to-fifteen million persons forcibly brought from West and West Central Africa to the various shores of the Americas were self-evident truths that we human beings could justify our evils. You shared with the framers of the United States Constitution a rightful distrust of the human capacity for good. You thought what the French social theorist Michel Foucault calls *governmentality*[10] had its limits too. Because our ancestors were caught up in the twisted machinations of power and greed as exploitable commodities, your skepticism about human enlightenment was ready-made.

Too many of your biographers see you as discovering the limitations of human rationality through the American theologian Reinhold Niebuhr. Taylor Branch in *Parting the Waters* beautifully narrates your relationship to Niebuhr. But you knew the shortcomings of human behavior long before you were introduced to Niebuhr's trenchant analysis. What Black child does not grow up learning that political power without restriction is horrendous? The lessons of the lynch mob and unbridled policing are that the power of human collectivity often goes awry. While you grew up relatively privileged, you were not immune from the crushing burden of being Black in a society conditioned to anti-Blackness. Before you read Niebuhr, you had lived these lessons. Niebuhr's theological theorization was important to you, but it was your Black experience that created your affinity with his pessimism. Your Blackness shaped the realpolitik behind your poetic idealism. Your family's personal history of enslavement had taught you that vile collective behavior was the sin to be resisted.

It was your religious faith that prevented you from totally descending into Machiavellian cynicism. Niccolò Machiavelli's *The Prince* is frequently read as though it is a primer for brutish use of political power. However, his work might be better read as a political tragedy about the unreliability of political leaders to maintain the transparent government that democracies require.[11] Manipulating governmental processes is too great a temptation for political leaders to withstand. Machiavelli, in a comic-tragic sort a way, held out hope that the ruler might reinstate democratic rule. However, the ex-slave and American abolitionist Frederick Douglass, some four hundred years later, accessed this political truth like Machiavelli: power rarely, if ever, concedes without a fight.

What occurred in Montgomery was just one movement among thousands of movements for independence. In April of 1955, approximately nine months before Ms. Rosa Parks's public refusal to move on a local bus became fixed in our memories, the Afro-Asian Conference, otherwise known as the Bandung Conference, took place in Bandung, Indonesia. Representatives of two-thirds of the world's people gathered to discuss the meaning of independence and democracy on their own terms. Montgomery's Black community was swept up in the moment along with those whom W. E. B. Du Bois called the "darker races," the vast majority of the world's people who desired to create their own new national democracies and economic distribution. From Montgomery to Bandung the desire was the same: a decent life, education for their children, and the promise of a government of their own choosing. It was a hopeful time, even if European powers, allied with the United States, used all available political machinations to hold onto exploitive rule in Asia and Africa.

Those optimistic days did not hide the brutishness. Powerful interests never voluntarily forfeit their dominance, as Douglass warned. Neither do they wish to be held accountable. The powerful apply a beastly calculus that their money or well-financed armies can exhaust resisters. We see it daily. They calculate that murder is the cheapest solution to dissension. They believe if they call a lie the truth, no one will know that it is subterfuge. The powerful know it is easy to buy even the most loftily educated—research scientists, social scientists, and historians. For the right price, injustice can be "objectively" explained. So there were coups, assassinations, wars, trumped-up charges, and false imprisonments. The Cold War, as it was euphemistically called, was hot. It was filled with landmines strewn across the globe—Egypt, the Gold Coast, Guatemala, Guinea, Iran, Kenya, Korea, and Vietnam. The Color Curtain, as the writer Richard Wright observed reporting from Bandung, was far more insidious and covered a greater part of the world than Winston Churchill's Iron Curtain.[12] It extended from Montgomery, the former capital of the slavocracy, to Washington, DC, London and Paris to Hanoi and Johannesburg. The Montgomery bus boycott was tied to a wider global struggle.[13]

Politicians, as you learned in Atlanta and Montgomery, are the creations of culture and cupidity. This chicken-and-egg dilemma is never-ending. Another way of seeing this is that Southern politicians used classic Freudian displacement theory. That is, to hide their deleterious economics from all Southerners, they used racial bigotries—the sine qua non of the South—as a scapegoat. And this tactic has only grown as racial demographics have shifted in the country. In the United States, politicians seek seats of local governance to maintain power and placate their White constituents with placebos that equate democracy with White hierarchy. Pointedly this means keeping the *niggers in their place* lest the rest of White America discover they are exploitable niggers too. Rhetorically it allows politicians to paper over the vexatious contradictions of capitalism, because they have niggers as perennial scapegoats. This is why slavery lasted so long in the United States. This is why the US version of apartheid remained for ninety years! And this is why sexism, which buttresses all these institutions, is wittingly deployed. This is true in Southern politics as it is throughout the country.

In today's world, there is willful undermining of democratic institutions by sundry political leaders, from clergy to elected officials. Democracy as an inner value of human dignity has been all but forgotten. Too many politicians have grown impatient with the process of haggling and negotiating that democracy requires. Too many religious leaders hold to a narrow zealotry about whose faith is pure and whose is not. Too many business leaders have drunk the hemlock of efficiencies, spreadsheets, and profit maximization rather than long-term investments. Too many spiritual leaders view the spirit as a tool to manipulate larger followings instead of a way of inculcating wise principles of community building.

Contemporarily around the globe, the militarized strongman, the uniform party, and the giant corporate conglomerates override our deliberations. This is not something new. Slavery in the US imperiled democratic governance from its inception. What is different, perhaps, is that globally we are being fooled into believing that efficient distribution of consumer goods is equivalent to being democratic. Surely one must realize that brand loyalty does not help us to deliberate or govern ourselves. Tragically, being a citizen is too often conflated with consumerism. Government is viewed as a delivery service, not a deliberative body of social good. What is worse is the marketing of fear. The consistent stampede of "moral panics" is worldwide. Fearmongering works. And the more we fear, the more we are convinced to run into the embrace of authoritarian leaders rather than self-governing collectively.

You called us to put away our fears, even though Southern political leaders ramped up fear by calling you a communist instigator. They were aghast that you recognized that they were naked emperors. They called for your head, but you stood your ground. You called for Black people to enact democracy and overthrow one-party rule, whether in Chicago or Montgomery. Nothing is ever pure about political struggle. Living democratically means living with ambiguities. The kind of democracy you preached requires us to recognize different voices, even ones that bring us discomfort. We must argue and ponder truths aloud. And this is the hardest thing to do. We all have our own comforting truths. In a democracy, however, we are expected to rub up against each other and concede space to one another. We must wrestle with great moral quandaries and give regard to competing notions of the good: tradition versus self-expression, individualistic pursuits versus communal order. You recognized democratic high ideals are never static; they are always in friction with other ideals that live in our society.

Today your highest ideals are being trampled on. From the over one hundred years of struggle to enfranchise all citizens of the US to the most mundane claims of personal freedoms, we are in a struggle to vouchsafe democracy. Political leaders resigned themselves to manipulative legalities instead of public debate over the merit of laws. Many of us wonder incredulously if we are truly at the end of history. Francis Fukuyama argued in *The End of History and the Last Man* that liberal democracy would grow across the globe and is the final or best form of government for all nations.[14] What Fukuyama did not realize—and what the history of Black struggle teaches us—is that there is nothing organic about liberal democracy. Democracies in all forms are not organic; they must be constantly maintained and kept in line. The United States from its inception was an exclusive democracy for elite Anglo-American males. It was American Africans, the most marginalized and ignored by US democracy, who pushed the country toward inclusive freedoms. As the spokesperson for the Montgomery bus boycott, you, and those you represented, had a democratic faith in the urgency of your own liberties. In our openly anti-democratic age, populist movements exchange this positive faith to reactionary ends. This is why we all must constantly scrutinize our democratic ideals. The perennial danger for democracies is manipulation and cooptation by a powerful minority. Alexis de Tocqueville had it wrong about America: it is not the tyrannical majority that can debase democracy; it has always been the tyrannical minority—the oligarchs whose outsized sense of themselves is destructive.

Amid this you asked the people of Montgomery to resist cynicism. This was also the genius of your oratory. You reminded the faithful that the struggle was worthwhile. Your words helped them, and continue to help us now, to see that democracy was big enough for all of us to thrive. As the consummate preacher, you aimed to change laws and reach beyond constitutional mandates to ambitiously promote human rights. You tried to persuade us that human ennoblement was worth the battle even as you recognized the "difficult days ahead."[15] This is the crowning achievement that made you and the protesters of Montgomery world-historical. Community and togetherness overtook self-interest.

The framers of the United States Constitution got the legalities of a democratic process partially right—right enough for them to compromise with one another and establish a racially exclusive democracy. But this was a compromise among one class of people, rather than one between all those in the new nation. They consciously, though stealthily, promoted vile enrichments from enslavement. Feverishly they employed colonial thuggery to remove Indigenous nations across North America. You observed in your 1964 book, *Why We Can't Wait*:

> Our nation was born in genocide when it embraced the doctrine that the original American, the Indian, was an inferior race. Even before there were large numbers of Negroes on our shores, the scar of racial hatred had already disfigured colonial society. From the sixteenth century forward, blood flowed in battles of racial supremacy. We are perhaps the only nation which tried as a matter of national policy to wipe out its Indigenous population. Moreover, we elevated that tragic experience into a noble crusade. Indeed, even today we have not permitted ourselves to reject or feel remorse for this shameful episode. Our literature, our films, our drama, our folklore all exalt it.[16]

Though nationalistic myths attempt to obscure it, this is our shared history. These ghostly power struggles haunt us. We cannot forget this history. It stands as a reminder of the things we do not wish to re-create. As you understood, vicious, instrumental uses of power can never create a free society. So we vigilantly stand guard against devious legalities that only offer freedoms for a few. True freedom has always meant more.

As a movement participant, you were in a queue of freedom struggles, as are we. Your high ideals stemmed from a lineage of religious and secular abolitionists. Recollecting your ideals reminds me that the social order we desire is one "at peace itself."[17] That is to say, one made up of transparent governance that seeks just adjudications for all of us—a society that does not trample over the rights of the have-nots, one that gives the unheard a hearing and accords recognition to the unseen. This is our highest ethical ideal.

3

A REVOLUTION OF VALUES

The revolution will not be televised
Will not be televised
Will not be televised
Will not be televised
—Gil Scott-Heron,
"The Revolution Will Not Be Televised"

Martin,

You called for "a revolution of values."[1] That was 1967, the year before the assassin's bullet catapulted you off your feet, severed your artery, and left you dead in a pool of blood. All that year you called for the overhaul of our national values. You argued that the combination of scientific technology and vast capital were endangering the lives of ordinary working people, especially Black people. Automation, beginning with the cotton picker, had undermined Southern agricultural laborers. Unbridled capitalism was destructive, and the moguls controlling industry could no longer be forced to negotiate with labor. You anticipated our era's technological bravado. "We must rapidly begin the shift from a 'thing'-oriented society to a 'person'-oriented society," you argued. This was prescient, but it went unheeded.

In fact, today's algorithmic robber barons have less moral reasoning than their nineteenth-century counterparts. In the previous era, Protestant theology held minimal sway on the Carnegies and the Rockefellers. Today there are no great moral institutions, not universities or houses of worship. Your observation was correct: "machines and computers, profit motives and property rights are considered more important than people."[2] Contemporary moguls share an extended history with the double-entry bookkeepers in the seventeenth century who accounted for human beings being carried across the Atlantic into the Americas. They were libertarian too. This is why the eighteenth-century Scotsman Adam Smith found it necessary in *Wealth of Nations,* his liberal guidebook to economics, that capitalism have a "moral economy." His common-sense view was that ordinary people could think for themselves about economics. He challenged elitists' notions that royals should solely determine the economic order.[3] However, very few modern economists discuss why he so openly worried about the morality of capitalism. For Smith the market best served when all were free to exercise their personal autonomy. It is ironic that he wrote as the transatlantic slave trade was in full bloom. He knew that the Scottish and English elite gained the wealth of nations by suppressing the personal autonomy of Africans cramped upon ships. Those elites then justified their wealth as being good for the people, as do today's elites.

Today, the deceased writer Ayn Rand is enshrined as the goddess of the market place.[4] Selfishness has replaced service as our reigning piety. Individuality has been bastardized into unmoored individualism. Adam Smith's philosophy, rooted in a communitarian theology, has now been fully atomized. It is unrecognizable. Rand's totalizing selfishness is now the first principle of the would-be monied class. This philosophical individualism is yoked to your description of "the giant triplets of racism, materialism and militarism," the Holy Trinity of US governance.[5] This is why you called for a "revolution in values." You believed that these nationalistic ambitions of conquest, expulsion, and debased labor—those values that established the US—could not be sustained. The promise of the Declaration of Independence was a statement of faith, a creed that Thomas Jefferson penned while his enslaved laborers kept Monticello's hearths stoked. Jefferson's contradictions were, as you knew, self-evident. Nevertheless, you demanded that we "rise up and live the true meaning of its creed,"[6] democracy's highest values.

You first used the phrase "revolution of values" in your 1967 book, *Where Do We Go from Here: Chaos or Community?* Throughout the 1960s, revolutions commenced everywhere. As you were writing, there was an enthusiasm for Martinican psychiatrist Frantz Fanon's 1961 book, *The Wretched of the Earth*, which also advocated revolution. Some of your slightly younger counterparts had grown weary of taking murderous blows. They were fatigued by your use of redemptive suffering as a framework in fighting US apartheid. In 1963, during the Birmingham campaign, *Wretched* was published. By the time of the Selma campaign in 1965, the compelling argument put forward by *Wretched* had seized the intellectual moment. To younger activists, the publication of *Wretched* could not have been timelier.

Fanon's book is a searing review of the tolls of European extractive colonial violence. Colonial rule, whether direct or indirect, impoverished two-thirds of the world's people. In *Wretched* Fanon calls attention to this violence and justifiably argues that people living under oppressive conditions must use violence themselves to gain freedom. Fanon was not a facile thinker; he was a trained psychiatric physician and a former student of Aimé Césaire, one of the founding members of the anticolonial movement known as Négritude. Fanon wanted healing from the psychic duress caused by colonial oppression. You both were generational contemporaries. And, in fact, you both resisted governmental power as an avenue to psychic wholeness for people living under oppression. You famously stated: "Whenever men and women straighten their backs up, they are going somewhere, because a man can't ride your back unless it is bent."[7]

I do not wish to belabor the point, but in defense of Fanon's violent ideas, France waged a brutal war to keep the Algerians colonized (in ways that parallel Saudi Arabia's oppression of Yemen now). Though historians often fail to connect these events, the French invasion in Algeria had a great deal to do with the French defeat in Haiti—a defeat equivalent to boxer Mike Tyson being beaten by his opponent Buster Douglas. The French feared that no other people of color would bow before their throne after the defeat in Haiti. Nevertheless, France kept up its Napoleonic grand illusion even after Haiti's gruesome resistance pried off France's kleptomaniac fingers. Licking their wounds, the French resumed their imperialistic fantasies in 1830 in Algeria, a conquest that redeemed the French among their competitors. And as we know from the post–Civil War South, there's nothing more heinous than redemption. The politics of redemption is always reactionary. Violence ensued, not because the people of Algeria wanted it, but because France's governing class needed to display their virility. It was sexual, as Fanon recognized. He did not capitulate to violence for its own sake. Violence was constitutive of imperialism. His question then was *How could the wretched reclaim their humanity in this oppressed situation?* He deemed it necessary to take up the sword. His question is a globally shared one; it was the same one asked by our enslaved foreparents.[8]

Clearly, Martin, there were limits to Fanon's thought. Overthrows rarely solve problems of governance or distribution of privilege and wealth. They seldom usher in "the kingdom of heaven." And as you stated, "The line of demarcation between defensive violence and aggressive violence is very thin." Armed violence begets revenge, not just democracies. "The ultimate weakness of violence is that it is a descending spiral, begetting the very thing it seeks to destroy. Instead of diminishing evil, it multiplies it."[9] Fanon's reflection on the dismal psychology of constant political self-effacement rightly described the logical anger and madness, but it was not a manual in securing the rights of vulnerable people. He did not need to keep the high moral ground as you felt your religion required you to do. Nor did he think through democratic options after revolution. It was your theological humanism that tempered you when it came to political violence. Though Fanon wrote with clarity on political violence, his reasoning left little insight as to how to govern in its aftermath.

You and your small army of nonviolent shock troops knew what coercive power looked like too. You faced violent treachery throughout the South. Lives and livelihoods were under constant threat. However, unlike Fanon, you were trying to win a White majority over to a minority coalition. Unlike his anticolonial struggle, in which the majority of Algerians desired political autonomy from France, your fight was as a minority in the middle of an empire. The civil rights battles were different. The movement had to persuade a White majority that systematic political exclusion was not in the best interest of the country.

You also differed because you believed violently led revolutions too often fail. And you had a point. Brutalized people often become brutalizers. Historically, when wars end, violence does not dissipate. Traumatic memories continue to fuel hateful feuds. We in the United States overendorse the use of violence. "Through violence you may murder the liar," you observed. "But you cannot murder the lie, nor establish the truth. Through violence you may murder the hater, but you do not murder hate. In fact, violence merely increases hate."[10]

This was your contention in opposing the United States' war in Vietnam. You eloquently explained how street violence, which besieges Black communities, decimates institutions, trust, and overall well-being. The paramount question that racked your brain was why violence was so normalized in our society. You stated aloud:

> As I have walked among the desperate, rejected, and angry young men, I have told them that Molotov cocktails and rifles would not solve their problems. I have tried to offer them my deepest compassion while maintaining my conviction that social change comes most meaningfully through nonviolent action. But they ask—and rightly so— what about Vietnam? They ask if our own nation wasn't using massive doses of violence to solve its problems, to bring about the changes it wanted. Their questions hit home, and I knew that I could never again raise my voice against the violence of the oppressed in the ghettos without having first spoken clearly to the greatest purveyor of violence in the world today—my own government.[11]

The militarism utilized in Vietnam is not that dissimilar from the violence that occurs on our overpoliced, cracked streets. Your lamentation about what was happening in Vietnam is now true domestically. It is easy to buy cheap military armament. Daily shootings are seedlings of strange fruit. The violence justified in Vietnam now perennially blooms on our poorest streets. Sadly, you were prophetic: the violence seems unending. The weapons of war have arrived at our doorsteps.

We have romanticized violence in our culture for too long. When President Harry S. Truman unleashed the first nuclear weapon, the jig was up. Every putative leader now craves nuclear weaponry. Pride, vanity, and revenge all factor into holding massively destructive power. The military threat of overwhelming violence may stay the peace, but it will never keep it. Hate and vengeance are a monstrous hydra.

And too many of the world's people are brutalized by militaristic sadism. For them there are no chivalrous rules to obfuscate savageries. Justifications do not matter. An eye for an eye! Jesus saves! The will of Allah! Broken treaties! Bogus territorial claims! Economic necessity! No matter the justifications, the yields are the same: death and destruction.

What is troublesome is that so many of us believe violence is virtuous. Militarism has been sacralized in honor codes and holy writs, and those that armies claim to protect, the "wretched of the earth," are the sacrifices in this ritual of devotion to military might. We tell ourselves that women are being protected by heroic valor, yet rape is a weapon of war used to debase communities. Young people working on our streets selling drugs are called *soldiers* as though being a warrior is not a tragedy. We forget that child soldiers are kidnapped and forced into disastrous wars. They are victimized to consolidate the privileges of adult males. Racist cynicism was the bright shining lie that justified war in Vietnam. You diagnosed the spread of gangrene within our political institutions. You were right: "it is time to break the silence" on our love affair with violence.[12]

This diet of human violence contributes to violent abuses of our planet. The results are vast human and species migration. Immigrants and refugees risk themselves on porous rafts. They are squeezed in freight trucks as human cargo. Like our forebearers they, too, are experiencing a great migration. They are fleeing brutalities, deprivations, scorched earth, and perverse predations. They move like all migrants move: from one old city neighborhood to another, from one suburb to the cheapest exurb, from one town to the next. They caravan across deserts and cross borders stealthily looking for a peaceable place to call their own.

In response, you proposed revolutionary nonviolence over facile warfare and violent sloganeering. While you were deeply empathetic with younger movement participants who desired a complete orbital change in United States politics, you thought that a Guevarist, Maoist, or even George Washingtonian revolution within the country was a fruitless endeavor. Logistically, a resistance group could not commandeer and continuously manufacture armaments. Self-defense on an individual basis is one thing, but a long-term armed struggle against a standing military demands that one control the production of armament. This was why John Brown's body still "lies a moldering in the grave": Brown's failure at Harpers Ferry was his desperate gambit to capture arms. We remember Brown's defeat because it foreshadowed the greater violence that was to come in the United States' Civil War, but desperadoes like the romantic Brown are rarely successful. Admittedly there is something thrilling and seductive about waging war. Yet it is important to remember that even the American revolutionaries, who were forming a government, were lucky themselves to have French intervention. In all actuality, standing armies, drones, and nuclear weaponry are too blunt to settle political differences. The only winners in armed struggles are bankers and arms dealers. Etymologically, capital plus arms equates to blood money. The former American president Dwight David Eisenhower called it "the military-industrial complex."

Your call for a revolution in values was on point. We must constantly give reflection as to how we should govern ourselves. What are the rules? What are our material impulses? How do we place limits on them? How do we prevent what you call the "thing-ification,"[13] or objectification, of one another? Radical political change requires us to think more deeply and consider what actual livable communities require.

However, there is also a danger in what you call a revolution of values. Values like the term *virtue* are too unsubstantial. Values can be cleverly perverted by society's puppet masters. Those in power also argue for values. The economic elite manipulates democratic impulses through commercial advertisements. "Revolution in values," like your phrase "content of our character," are easily muddled. They are twisted to uphold the status quo and wealthy interests rather than the interests of the many. Ironically, they are used to justify the very violent behavior you politically opposed.

This plutocratic control leaves the laboring poor living off a coarse diet. The poorest of the laboring classes are left exhausted, parasitically feeding off their neighbors. Henry David Thoreau claimed that the "mass of men lead lives in quiet desperation. What is called resignation is confirmed desperation."[14] What he did not say, and perhaps should have, is that desperation does not always remain quiet. It builds and episodically explodes—in peasant revolts and urban rebellions. Those revolts are "the voices of the unheard,"[15] but they are not strategically aimed to make political change.

Black freedom struggles were born of unfree labor, and we must always be cognizant that our revolutionary values are not in and of themselves sufficient to keep democracy alive. Any cursory look at US life is an instruction manual on the pitfalls of democratic practices. As Ella Baker urged, "We who believe in freedom cannot rest."[16] What is truly revolutionary is the daily effort. Democracy necessitates a never-ending refurbishment, not a one-time overthrow of a powerful regime. This is what I believe you meant by "a revolution in values." You knew that if politics were not infused with a critically informed consciousness, they quickly festered into manipulations. As you knew from the Baptist ministry, values are conveniently engineered to hide cynical quests for personal riches using emotional appeals to spirituality.

You, however, remained a committed democrat. The beginning of your understanding of revolutionary values commenced from your theological analysis of the human condition. "Be ye transformed by the renewing of your minds," is from the Apostle Paul's Epistle to the Romans. I agree that the first act in any revolution is the transformation of our minds. However mindful any of us might become, a democratic revolution is a collective action. It requires a never-ending devotion to the actual building of a free and open democratic society. Reconciliation of peoples is the aim of a truly freedom-loving nation. Fanon's call for revolution was justifiable given the inflexibility of Gaullist France. The nettlesome aspect of his thinking, however, was there was no room for reconciliation. The struggle in Algeria went on from 1954 to 1962 and caused an estimated 1.5 million Algerians their lives. In 1956, the year Hungarians protested the domination of the Soviet Union, the people of Montgomery defied the scourges of racial segregation with self-governing ardor. As you noted in your speech "The Birth of a New Age," revolution is a new birth that must be guided by two intertwined principles of reconciliation and justice.

> As we move in this transition from the old age into the new we will have to rise up in protest. We will have to boycott at times, but let us always remember that boycotts are not ends within themselves. A boycott is just a means to an end. A boycott is merely a means to say, "I don't like it." It is merely a means to awaken a sense of shame within the oppressor but the end is reconciliation. The end is the creation of a beloved community.[17]

4

LIKE A KING

Well Martin's dream
Has become Rodney's worst
Nightmare.
—BEN HARPER, "LIKE A KING"[1]

Martin,

The first time I heard Ben Harper's song "Like a King," I was struck by its parallelism, the juxtaposition of the two Kings.

Harper was not the first to sing about you. On April 5, 1968, the day after your assassination, Chicago blues–great Otis Spann, backed up by Muddy Waters and his band, went to a storefront church and recorded two songs, "Hotel Lorraine" and "Blues for Martin Luther King." From the latter:

Oh, did you hear the news?
Coming out of Memphis, Tennessee, yesterday
Yes, fellow, I know you had to've heard the news
That happened down in Memphis, Tennessee, yesterday.[2]

Over fifty years later the recording still feels immediate. Spann captured the rawness of grief felt on Chicago's South and West Sides. His twelve-bar blues intoned the sorrowfulness of that moment so powerfully that I still feel the pain of it when I cue it up to play.

Nina Simone's song "Why? (The King of Love Is Dead)" was also performed within days of your assassination. In it, she wonders what the future will be without you.

> What's gonna happen now? In all of our cities?
> My people are rising; they're living in lies,
> Even if they have to die.[3]

Simone's grief-filled song played angrily over the airwaves of Los Angeles in the community that suckled Rodney King as a toddler. She, like all of us, was disillusioned with a country that permitted your murder.

Simone's song was soon followed up by one recorded by Dion titled "Abraham, Martin and John," which was written in the wake of Robert Kennedy's assassination in June of 1968. His recording laments your death as it sentimentalizes your life, along with the lives of Lincoln and Kennedy. Dion's recording wistfully sweeps away Black communal anger and the controversial history associated with Lincoln's and Kennedy's politics. "Has anybody here seen my old friend Martin? Can you tell me where he's gone?"[4] Wistfully, it is a song about good men with dreams who die too early.

In 1970, Nancy Dupree's "Docta King" recorded an evocative nostalgia. Her refrain, like Simone's, contrasts your praxis of love with your violent murder:

> Oh, how it hurts me.
> The man was pure as a baby's breath.

His words were love and brotherhood, . . .
And they shot him down.[5]

In 1980, Stevie Wonder filled the airwaves with an up-tempo, reggae-inflected, celebratory anthem called "Happy Birthday." Wonder's song led the way in establishing a federal holiday in honor of you.[6] Twelve years after your death, Wonder filled us with joyous nostalgia about your activism.

> I just never understood
> How a man who died for good
> Could not have a day that would
> Be set aside for his recognition.[7]

Eleven years later, Wonder's song would find a hard-edged counterpoint in hip-hop group Public Enemy's rap "By the Time I get to Arizona." When it was released in 1991, there was no joyous sentimentality left. Black people were angry. Arizona's political leadership had rejected your named holiday, a decision that was a racist dog whistle. Public Enemy's emcee, Chuck D, rhymes:

> This ain't no damn dream,
> Gotta know what I mean,
> It's team against team,
> Catch the light beam.[8]

Following Public Enemy, Ben Harper conjured up you and Rodney King in 1994. Harper's song came in the wake of the 1991 beating of Rodney King and the ensuing Los Angeles rebellion. Lyrically, Harper grasps "the difficult days ahead,"[9] after the four police officers, whom the entire world saw unrelentingly beating the subdued King, were stunningly acquitted. The cops acted as frenzied villagers defending themselves from a possessed mytho-logical behemoth. Like those who justified lynch mob justice, the people of Simi Valley justified the officers' criminality. In Harper's song you were summoned to the scene, this time twenty-nine years after your visit to L.A.'s Watts neighborhood in the aftermath of a different rebellion.

In 1965, you walked through L.A.'s smoldering Burned-over District. During that visit your philosophy was openly questioned. Whether you liked it or not, you had been coronated the king of the movement. Even though you were still young yourself, in your midthirties, many young people there, especially young men, viewed you as an old-school representative. Your demeanor exem-plified their parents' generation, those Arkansans, Louisianans, Okies, and Texans who migrated westward in a spiritual caravan every bit as powerful as the one Latter-Day Saints elder Brigham Young led. Their spiritual succor sustained them through agricul-tural toil and political humiliation. Their children growing up in the West faced an urban apartheid, set in legal codes of employ-ment, housing, and lending, every bit as ugly as what they left in the South. The personal and economic isolation was even harsher. You observed "the Negro lives on a lonely island of poverty in the midst of a vast ocean of material prosperity."[10] Although you had analyzed the severity of Black economic exclusion, your personal southern-preacher style was not as urbane as Malcolm's zoot-suit, streetwise style.[11] You did not possess the hardness of the Nation of Islam's prison spirituality and did not, on the surface, appear angry enough. In an essay, Julius Lester called these city rebels "the angry children of Malcolm X," today's Black Lives Matter activists' grandparents.[12]

In 1961, Malcolm X found himself following your strategy. He filed a lawsuit against the Los Angeles police force for the murder of a member of the Nation of Islam. Malcolm showed as much restraint as you in his use of the courts. He tempered his rhetoric and followed legal procedures. The younger generation, especially men, figured that you did not understand the brute game of urban politics and thus admired the formerly incarcerated Harlemite more. In hindsight, they misjudged you and Malcolm alike.[13]

Harper's song imagines that your presence might have ame-liorated the fate of Rodney King and the L.A. rebellion, like you did at Watts. As "the moral leader of our nation," as A. Philip Randolph dubbed you during the March on Washington for Jobs and Freedom, your presence as spokesperson of the movement was required at all outbreaks of rebellion by Black people. Both the Watts and L.A. rebellions were driven by economic divestiture and brutal policing. Leading up to Watts, Black and White southerners had journeyed West to pursue greater economic opportunities, many landing in L.A. The White migrants brought with them a segregationist ethic that was established in the city's suburbs and exurbs. "Like a King" beautifully compresses history, but contrary to Harper's creation, when you arrived in any city, your leader-ship was limited. The political playground you exercised in was always jealously monitored by your political allies, rivals, and the all-seeing eyes of state security.

In 1965, in your *Saturday Review* article "Beyond the Los Angeles Riots," you anticipated the injustice that Rodney King suffered. You wrote:

> In these terms Los Angeles could have expected riots because it is the luminous symbol of luxurious living for whites. Watts is closer to it, and yet farther from it, than any other Negro community in the country. The looting in Watts was a form of social protest very common through

the ages as a dramatic and destructive gesture of the poor toward symbols of their needs.[14]

Twenty-four years later Rodney King was your dream turned nightmare. His experience was closer to the tortured reality of Chaym Smith in Charles Johnson's underappreciated novel *Dreamer*.

Johnson's novel is creatively plotted. It centers on three fictional characters in your circle. The first is Matthew Bishop, an earnest college dropout, who is a dedicated follower of yours and a worker in the movement. Matthew narrates the story. He is a budding philosopher of religion (like Johnson himself), constantly assessing your activism.

The second character is Chaym Smith, your look-alike. His name Chaym is the Hebrew word for "life" (also transliterated as Chayyim or Chaim). Matthew discovers that the name Chaym is an etymological variation of Cain, Adam and Eve's son who murders his twin brother, Abel. Through the novel Johnson uses Chaym Smith to explore whether one life can stand in for another. Leaning on Buddhist thought, Johnson asks what makes a life significant. Or as Chaym emphatically tells Matthew, chastising him, "Do what you gotta do, Bishop. One thing I've always believed, you don't *have* to do what anybody else does. Only what *you* have to do. Ain't no two people on this planet got the same fuckin' *dharma*."[15] By this, he means we all have individual paths through suffering. Each of us must face up to the transitory nature of human existence. In Buddhism, enlightenment comes from ridding oneself of egotistical dissatisfactions. Right living and nirvana, in a world of suffering and impermanence, come from a life that is cherished. In Buddhism the self is imaginary.

The third character in the novel is Amy, Johnson's least developed character. She is Bishop's lover and a dutiful laborer in the struggle. Amy is truly selfless. She is the only female protagonist in the story and interestingly does not possess a last name. Perhaps she represents the countless Black women whose unsung civil rights activism is still rarely credited. Bishop, Chaim, and Amy make an unlikely trio in supporting you during your last two years of life.

The story is set in Chicago and Southern Illinois, following your real-life struggles against the city's Byzantine politics. At that time, Chicago was controlled by Cook County Democratic Party chairman and mayor, Richard J. Daley, the Boss. Neither you nor your lieutenants had faced power politics so steeped in corporate businesses and multiethnic patronage. The Black/White politics of Birmingham had been challenging, but nothing rivaled Chicago.

In the South you recognized the clergy were pawns of the White supremacist Citizens' Councils, but Chicago was a city where everyone was pawn-brokered by "the machine," as it was called. Mayor Daley constantly frustrated the movement in Chicago, and he knew how to strategically capture the news cycle, leaving you no room to dramatize local injustices. Daley was one hundred times more powerful than your wiliest opponent in Albany, Georgia, police chief Laurie Pritchett. In 1963, *Time* magazine featured Mayor Daley on its cover with a story titled "Clouter with Conscience."[16] He was unconscionable to his Black constituents, even though Black voters helped him secure office. He owned the Black political establishment—politicians, preachers, and small business owners. Publicly they sang his hosannas, for they feared being cut off from the city's patronage. When you arrived in Chicago, six Black aldermen silently stood behind the mayor in a press conference as he stated there was no need for your presence in the city. This is how Daley reigned. It was "the city that works."[17]

I must admit, your SCLC Chicago campaign was noble but quixotic. And this is the beauty of Johnson's novel. It captures your emotional weariness as you press for democratic justice. This is where Bishop and Amy enter Johnson's tale. They try to get Chaim, your look-alike, to step in briefly and unobtrusively give you a much-needed respite. However, this is impossible. Chaim is a man with his own internal angry demons. No matter how much he might look like you, he cannot be you.

Even when vast numbers of Black folk disagreed with your principled belief in nonviolence, they loved you. You put your life on the line in their cause—our cause. Though Ella Baker, Diane Nash, Jo Ann Robinson, Bayard Rustin, and C. T. Vivian were all better organizers than you, your charisma was infectious. Johnson captures the zeitgeist beautifully.

> His critics were right—sometimes he was a damned poor organizer. But how could he oversee everything? Be every-where at once? He felt he was caught in a current sweeping him relentlessly forward, one in which he was drowning, unable to catch his breath or keep his head above water as the waves propelled him helplessly on like a man hurtling over Niagara Falls.[18]

From the mid-nineteenth to the twentieth century, German socialist thinkers like Karl Marx and Max Weber were preoccupied with charisma too. In Marx's rendering, though, there was no God-sanctioned charisma. He believed that true charisma arises from the collective. His idea was that there would be a govern-ing dictatorship driven by the proletariat, who were an advanced set of the working class. These proletarians would lead the way in reclaiming their labor for their own benefit and health. They would overthrow the industrial Caesars, the bourgeoisie, those large-scale capitalists who owned factories, banks, transportation, and financial instruments. The people, Marx believed, must not rely on any singular personality. It is their collectivity that shapes history. They must direct the rules of their political economy without any godlike projection.

The sociologist Max Weber tweaked Marx's idea that charisma arose from the proletariat. He viewed charisma as a sometimes-necessary component to building institutions and leading social movements. The benefit of charismatic leadership is that the gifted individual is able to persuade others to join protest movements. Charismatic leaders may represent the social aspirations of the oppressed or the resentful aggrieved. According to Weber, however, there is something impermanent about charismatic leadership, and the leader must eventually yield to those state operational apparatuses that control daily routines—legal enforcement, tax collection, and welfare distribution. When the charismatic leader fails, corrupt nepotism spreads like an unrelenting cancer. At that point, powerful persuasion cannot hold. Charisma can be easily manipulated and used to enflame the heart with vague promises of equitable solutions to national inequities. It can nefariously hide like the wizard behind the curtain in *The Wizard of Oz*. This is accomplished through our personal identification with the leader and a symbiosis of aspirations between a leader and their base of people.

Black American preachers astutely cultivated charisma through the use of musically intoned spoken word. They practice the art of moving and mobilizing followers. This tradition has often been criticized by those, like the secular, who cannot command the spoken word, often out of simple jealousy. Black religious charismatic leadership has been based on the ability to persuasively manifest hope. That has been the genius of the people called to preach the good news. These highly localized priests and priestesses of dreams knew their primary calling was to uplift their congregants and their needs. To do this, they had to be called by their people. Inherently, then, in this political relationship are tensions, a constant push and pull to control just how far charismatic leadership should go and exactly whose dreams are faithful to the realities of the people's circumstances.

Luckily for us your charisma was tempered. Hearing the voice of God within, you saw your duty (as any Baptist preacher would) as preaching persuasively to your congregation, which grew to be the nation and then the world. You used your charismatic authority wisely, always a preacher first:

> But before I was a civil rights leader, I was a preacher of the gospel. This was my first calling and it still remains my greatest commitment. You know, actually all that I do in civil rights I do because I consider it a part of my ministry. I have no other ambitions in life but to achieve excellence in the Christian ministry. I don't plan to run for any political office. I don't plan to do anything but remain a preacher.[19]

You and Rodney shared last names, but your lives were not the same. And yet, your life, Rodney's, and our lives are woven together. Our interwoven lives raise profound questions about the immediate realities of living democratically in the United States: What can we hope for? What is politically possible? Are nation-states at an end? Is corporate feudalism our new plantations? Can our society abandon its dependency on racism? Like you, Rodney wanted to live without fear. He shared your dream to live in a democracy that offered him a livelihood and protection against racial injustice. "Can we all get along?" he pleaded.

In *Dreamer* Chaym listens to you from the wings of an Evanston, Illinois, African Methodist Episcopal church after failing to effectively imitate you. He learns a far deeper truth about you. Here Johnson, using his Buddhist-modulated philosophy, characterizes you as saying:

> After liberating lunch counters, winning court battles and homes in nice neighborhoods, we must in our next campaign free consciousness itself from fear, from what William Blake called "mind-forg'd manacles." But to do this we must unlearn things. We must be quiet and not deluded or deceived by the creation of our own minds. The soil of the soul must be plowed. . . . After a time, I tell you, a man comes to see only a We, this precious moment as a tissue in time holding past, future, and present, with all of us in the red, everlasting debtors—ontological thieves—in a universe of interrelatedness. . . . Every man and woman is a speculum, our mirror. Our twin.[20]

Johnson's description is powerful. We are all yoked together. His fictive telling reminds me that none of us can ever own or parrot you. We cannot resurrect you. Your time is not ours. Both you and Rodney are gone. Our struggle for a just society is a continuation of a historic quest to create a truly just and democratic nation. We face our own set of difficulties as we draw on the wisdom of the past and shape our present. The present belongs to us to seize. We are relational selves, not singular.

The goal of democratic struggle is to create political space where we live in better relationship to one another. There is no perfection, just series of negotiated solutions to limit brutalities, decrease hopelessness, and ameliorate suffering. Rodney King's question, "Can we all get along?" was one you perpetually sought answers to as well. In your graduate student days, you anticipated Rodney's question when you wrote:

Many, therefore, stand looking at the world's calamity as at a gigantic spectacle, feeling that the problem is well-nigh insoluble. I do not see how we can take that position, however, if we perceive what the gist of the world's problem really is: a lack of world brotherhood. I am convinced that if our civilization is to survive, we must rise from the narrow horizon of clashing nationalism to the wide horizon of world cooperation. No longer can we be content with a national ethical code, but instead we must have an international ethical code. . . . This is our great opportunity. This is our only hope.[21]

5

DRUM MAJOR INSTINCT

This a battle of the bands, this a drum break
Majorettes on the school yard
Where my drum majors? Pull out your bullhorn.
—Missy Elliot, "Pep Rally"

Deny it to a king? Then happy low, lie down!
Uneasy lies the head that wears a crown.
—William Shakespeare, *Henry IV*

Martin,

Leadership is wearisome, but so many believe they can wear the crown. This requires the type of stamina that few possess. Admiration is due to Britain's Queen Elizabeth II. For over sixty years she has been the symbol of what is supposed to be the best representation of her empire. Being a royal is quite unfathomable to me. Millions voyeuristically gobble up sensationalized tabloid pornography about them, though very few actually wish to live in their glass castles. Queen Elizabeth II is not the political or military leader of England that her namesake was. The contemporary queen can quietly suggest things to influence the various prime ministers, but she does not have to engage the ruckus of her Parliament and the unseemly side of divisive party politics. The rough and tumble of democratic politics are best left to the nastiness of the two major parties. This is a far cry from Elizabeth I's rule in Shakespeare's time.

In 1597, when *Henry IV* was first performed, Martin Luther, your namesake, had disrupted the sixteenth century. His challenge to Roman Catholicism's devotional, intellectual, and filial dominance fractured Europe's political map like Pangea. A new order of superstates had already been forming—the Ottomans to the east and Spain in the west. Luther's theological insurrection was followed by more radical protestant thinkers, forcing European monarchs to defend their rule. They declared jihads against protestant heresy. This religious revolution set off by your namesake crossed the Atlantic. Ships carrying varieties of dissenting protestants, impoverished debtors, and enslaved Middle Passengers were all shaded by Martin Luther's religious protest. It was an ideological linchpin for the Anglican colonization of North America. Luther's rhetorical challenge to the monarchical status of Roman Catholicism aided in igniting and keeping Europe ablaze for thirty years. This fire traveled across the Atlantic, and the same militarized mentalities that scorched northern Europe subdued Indigenous nations throughout the Americas. Eventually these émigrés of English dissidence and their descendants wielded enough power to challenge England's monarchical sovereignty and replace it with the people's rule. They exchanged lifelong lords with elected representation. And they boldly declared themselves to be the United States.

Leadership, whether for or in opposition to the status quo, is burdensome. Arduous choices must be made. The irony is that there's an innate human desire, often an inane one, to be seen as a leader or have the privileges of living in a leader's immediate shadow. The "drum major instinct" was a sermon you cribbed and gave your own improvisational voice.[1] It describes well how many of us want to be the lead majorette, the point guard, the striker, the CEO—or simply the HNIC! It is instinctual to all of us. Many of us try to sustain humility, but truthfully, we all want to be seen leading the pack. Few of us escape it.

In 1970, the writer John A. Williams attempted to demystify the messianism that surrounded your legacy. *The King God Didn't Save* is an intimate and eloquently cathartic rendering of grief about your human leadership. It caused a minor uproar at the time of its publication, just two years after your death. Now if the marketers of Williams's book had been more biblically savvy, they might have recognized that God did not save many kings from the political consequences of their actions. Most of the Jewish kings were quite troubled and judged critically. In comparison, you died a biblical prophet's death advocating for underpaid workers.

Williams's account of your last few years of life is a gripping read, but I find his assertion that you were puffed up by the press beginning with the Montgomery bus boycott a bit overstated. You had been voted as spokesperson for the Montgomery Improvement Association (MIA), and what caught the media's attention was how shrewdly photogenic and resolute you appeared to be. You were not puffed up on the scale perpetrated by William Randolph Hearst or anticommunist preacher Billy Graham. Your people puffed you up in Montgomery because you were their spokesperson.

You were not the commanding general barking orders but rather an organizer reacting to events beyond your control. In fact, the generals just below you were never fully compliant. There were young and driven comrades who frequently tried to usurp your position as national spokesperson. Stokely Carmichael (Kwame Ture) and Jesse Jackson Sr. sought the camera as much you did.

Roy Wilkins, the head of the NAACP, jealously guarded his organization's position in the movement. Wilkins at times appeared to be hopelessly out of touch with the community. He had an old man's disdain toward the youthful organizers on the ground. And then there was the leader of the National Urban League, Whitney Young, whose respectable ideals could not entreat elected officials away from Cold War intrigue toward mild economic reforms. But other than Mary McLeod Bethune and Marcus Garvey, very few Black leaders had a constituency of the day-in-and-day-out working folk.

Even recently, contemporary figures have fought to see who is most representative of your leadership. One such media hullabaloo occurred between Dr. Cornel West and former president Barack Obama over the use of your Bible for his second inauguration.[2] West correctly criticized Obama and reminded him that you were a critic of US racial imperialism. However, in 2009 Obama acquitted himself with Niebuhresque realpolitik in his Nobel Peace Prize acceptance speech, owning up to his role as commander in chief. He differentiated your role as a purveyor of hope from his as an activist with presidential responsibilities entangled in domestic and global machinations.[3] You assuredly would have been a thoughtful critic of the Obama presidency, as you were of both presidents Johnson and Kennedy. So, I sided with West's urgent feeling that Obama's good intention was in fact coopting critical resistance for state power. However, I felt that West dangerously tried to usurp your legacy as though he were you. This in my eyes was a blasphemy of another sort. Your legacy belongs to all of us. Freedom struggles never belong to any one individual. And we must always recollect you were called by your people, not your own charisma.

Saul Alinsky, the famed Chicago community organizer, frequently asked organizers "Who are your people?"[4] Organizing requires a base, and your base was churchgoing folk. Thus your organization was called the Southern Christian Leadership

Conference: it was Black, Christian, and southern. It reflected the best and worst about your base—the apprehensive conservatism, the misplaced hostilities, the prayerful vigilance, the political disfunction, the spiritual ecstasy, and the utter pettiness. Rooted in those country and urban churches that were built with Black dollars and hands, it was the people's own meager philanthropy. This was your base.

Leadership has a comedic element to it. It isn't always the most organized who attract followers. Organizational skills are important, but they do not guarantee that one will be an effective public leader. Leadership is judged by how well poetic dreams are articulated. By all historical accounts, Marcus Garvey was inept organizationally (Amy Ashwood was not, and she made him look better than he was); however, to his followers, he was a grand leader. Mary McLeod Bethune was organizationally and publicly a giant and beloved by her base, but she often remained hidden behind the veil of Jane Crow. So however faulty your critics found your leadership, your people saw your vision. It resonated with them and they came out of their pews and took to the streets.

People with liberal educational understandings often wonder why others who share their class status follow seemingly uninformed leaders. In reflection, these leaders are wily and not as incompetent or ignorant as they slyly pretend to be. Being unpolished and unapologetic is as performative as being in a P. T. Barnum circus. Reactionary populists understand their people's aspirations. They are attuned to their followers' fears as much as to their aspirations. They understand their base. Intellectuals have always been afraid of populist leaders. And there is a rightful fear that their reactionary leadership might develop into authoritarianism. Historically people have been fooled by wily populist leaders—Mussolini, Hitler, Jim Jones, and Benjamin "Pitchfork Ben" Tillman are deadly examples. These rhetorically skillful leaders know how to politically manipulate their bases. They urge people to destroy their neighbors.

However, you exercised different brands of populist leadership. You offered a constructive agenda. You asked people to take their Jesus seriously and take him into the streets in peaceful protest. Whatever can be said of your organizational strengths, you had a base committed to their freedom and the freedom of others. They were among the pious proletariat. They were the vanguard who toiled for low wages, disciplined their children, and prayed for them to have better lives than their own. Snobbish liberals and chic radicals mistakenly sneer at these pious people.

Sophisticates are too often hypercritical of Black cultural institutions. Truthfully it feels as though they do not like the civil society of Black people's own creation. For them, these institutions seem to get in the way, a distraction in addressing crime, disease, education, and matters of sexual exclusion. In their eyes, Black-led institutions like churches are retrograde. But these are the institutions where Black people unashamedly make their own worlds. They may not always affect state politics, but they affect communal politics. This was one of the reasons why so many Black church folk resisted facile talk about "racial integration." In their eyes, the term simply meant giving up their power over the systems they had democratically built. You gave voice to a moral discourse from inside your own community. Your articulation was not simply to please a predominantly White press corps. You gave articulation to a soul-searching, what the poet Elizabeth Alexander terms "Black interiority."[5] One of your theological mentors, Howard Thurman, called it "the inward journey."[6]

All politics begins provincially, in the village. These local spaces and affiliations—churches, Eastern Stars, Elks, Greeks, Jack and Jills, and the Prince Hall Freemasonry—are where the daily routines of life occur. In order to mobilize people, you took their own institutional life seriously. You were a part of your people's community fabric. You belonged to their institutions and understood them as an insider. Their institutions allowed them to survive distorting political systems. Daily structures of existence are not grand or national; they are pedestrian.

In your relationship to local institutions you saw an untapped power. You understood that there was a highly functioning democratic culture pulsing through the arteries of Black America, a culture that shunned the advice of elite tastemakers to create homegrown egalitarianism. Though you were an insider, you continued to expand your imagination to possibilities broader than the parochialism of the community you grew up in.

In this regard, your role as an orator is inestimable. There is always the danger of rhetoric without substance. The ancient Greeks worried aloud about sophistry, rhetorically pleasing but nonsubstantive arguments to win over an uncritical crowd. You used your rhetorical gifts to give meaning to the movement and the nation. Back in June of 1982, I attended the great antinuclear movement rally in Central Park. It was larger than the March on Washington, but I do not remember anything of substance that was said that day. No orator set the occasion. There was no showstopper, no poet to inspire. Too much can be made of rhetoric, but too little can be made of it too. A drum major sets and keeps the beat.

Being a drum major is difficult. You have to balance your own showboating desires for the betterment of the band. Drum majors easily become out of step. Leaders too often forget that they are servants to an end and not the end themselves. It is thrilling to see a drum major twirling and throwing the baton high in the sky and bending backward with her plumed hat touching the ground. However entertained the crowd might be by this performance, if the drum major dances too much, she will lose the band's groove, making her performance ineffectual.

Drum majors must be wary of too much adulation. It is a narcotic. Figuring out how to keep one's ego in check is the biggest responsibility of a democratic leader. Learning to constantly define and keep to the mission is the hardest balancing act. And it is important to remember that true leadership is never carried out in a vacuum. Leadership is carried out amid other leaders. Kings and queens lead with landed lords and court secretaries, preachers lead alongside deacons and elders, popes lead with bishops and cardinals, presidents govern with senators and representatives, and CEOs have a board of directors. The disciples had egos just as Jesus did. This is what makes drum majoring exhausting.

You had your share of fellow drum majors. You were surrounded by accomplished allies and frenemies. It is to your credit that you recognized their spheres. A greatness in your leadership was your generosity. You tried as best as you could to always be magnanimous to your peers. They were your fellow drum majors. Some envied your access to the national press. They often forgot that getting news coverage was the easy part and not all news was good news.

The Montgomery Improvement Association (MIA) provided the struggle that brought you public notoriety. Being the MIA spokesperson was a great vehicle to firmly cement your leadership of the Dexter Avenue Baptist Church. Your formidable predecessor was the Reverend Vernon Johns, and though sadly congregants dismissed him as their preacher for his inflammatory style of confronting the legal racism in Alabama, his legacy lives on today.[7] Even if some of the congregants feared Johns's challenge to segregationist rule, they recognized his courage. Surely Johns was the precedent to ACT UP, the HIV protest coalition of the 1980s. He advertised his sermon "It Is Safe to Murder Negroes in Montgomery" on the church's marquee.[8] Johns had no time for niceties. He challenged his educated congregation, including its middle-class pretentions of selling of fish after his Sunday sermons. He, like

Booker T. Washington, believed salaries from state jobs, such as a teacher, were not sufficient to build robust self-reliance. These jobs alone, he felt, kept his membership dependent on the White power structure that sought to control Black people in Montgomery. I imagine you wanted to differentiate your leadership from that of Johns's with the Dexter congregants. Unlike John Williams, I cannot blame you for quietly trying to set yourself up to be elected the spokesperson for the MIA.

I am sure you had no idea that leadership would demand so much from you. You thought that your protest would be similar to the one led in Baton Rouge, for which the Reverend T. J. Jemison won notoriety.[9] In 1953 the five-day June protest secured in Baton Rouge a more tolerable segregation and demonstrated the organizing model for what would take place in Montgomery. You had no idea what was coming. As a twenty-six-year-old you were out to make a name for yourself, not as your father's junior but as the young Reverend Doctor King. You quickly came to the realization that this movement was not about you.

Charisma, as you knew, is translated from Greek via Latin into English. In Greek, *kharisma* means "a talent or beauty from God or the gods." Christian theology would reshape this into an aspect of God's grace. The Apostle Paul argued that charisma did not belong to him but was Christ's work through him. Like Moses, he was bound to the one who gave him a new compact of faith. Charisma, Paul believed, must be bracketed by humility. A power lay beyond his own flawed mortality. It came from the resurrected Jesus, the Christ. Paul believed he was not seeking the adulation of the Caesar but was simply the carrier of the good news of the Christ. The Christ held the power to radically and eternally alter the lives of people even beyond Roman rule. His charisma was just one gift among the many gifts in the kingdom of Christ, just as yours was one among gifted organizers in the movement.

Now, do not misunderstand me. You had thought about justice throughout your graduate training, but you enjoyed the adulation that fame brought. Williams describes you as running to pick up the newspaper to read the flattering assessment of your leadership and becoming quite depressed when things that went awry were blamed on you. You knew that public perception was an important metric for the movement's success. There is a thin line between our egos and the office we hold. What is remarkable was how well you learned to subvert yourself to a greater cause. You tried your best to use your charisma to be democratically accountable to the movement.

In my estimation, your drum major style was Washingtonian. I do not mean Booker, though he was a powerfully effective leader; no, I mean George. His greatness was determined by his willingness to let go of the presidency to stabilize an unsteady republic through routine elections. Unlike that George, who went up against King George, you were not an elected state leader. Your leadership ran counter to the state. You were a preacher, a leader ordained by your people and their denominational body. Baptists were dissenters in England and throughout the southern colonies, and you embodied that tradition, more fully than White Baptists themselves. Even when you could have taken some of the Nobel Peace Prize winnings to support your family, you refused. You gave it all to the movement. This was the selfless crown you wore.

Leadership is thankless. Toward the end of your life, you were physically exhausted. Your voice grew raspier and your eyes were glazed from sleepless nights. You were weary of the coalitional infighting and the political gaming. You and Coretta had made extraordinary sacrifices for the cause, and your weariness was fully on display. You were tired.

Early in your life you learned about sacrifice in your Sunday school upbringing. Jesus stories were vivid reminders to you of what sacrifice meant. The hymns from the *National Baptist Hymn Book* were filled with songs like Thomas Shepherd's "Must Jesus Bear the Cross Alone."

> Must Jesus bear the cross alone
> And all the world go free?
> No there's a cross for everyone,
> And there's a cross for me.[10]

In 1987, author David Garrow's *Bearing the Cross: Martin Luther King, Jr., and the Southern Christian Leadership Conference* aptly borrowed from Shepherd's hymn for its title. What Garrow's book documented was the minutiae of your day-to-day sacrifices.[11] You were nurtured not with self-absorbing odes but with those sacrificial hymns such as George Bennard's "The Old Rugged Cross":

> So I'll cherish the old rugged cross
> Till my trophies at last I lay down.
> I will cling to the old rugged cross
> And exchange it someday for a crown.[12]

Jesus, you learned, led a poor people's campaign against a recalcitrant Palestinian monarchy, puppeteered by Roman imperialism. As a rule, the Romans crucified political insurgents, so Jesus was always your example of what could happen when waging a struggle against the powerful. Leaders of the dispossessed must be ready to sacrifice and be sacrificed. Your swollen liver at the time of your death demonstrated your sacrificial stresses; physically you were a ticking time bomb. Being a drum major always looks more glamorous than it really is.

The Hebrew scriptures were part of your story too, just as they were for your dear friend Rabbi Abraham Joshua Heschel. You frequently preached on Israel's royals—Ahab, David, Saul, and Solomon. The beauty of the Hebrew Bible is that these kings were openly acknowledged as flawed. You lived with terrible shame about your sex life outside your marriage, even though the biblical kings were more rapscallion than you ever were. Their prophets outed them for their injustices and not their escapades, as the FBI and some in the US press attempted to do to you.

Your friend and fellow activist Vincent Harding wrote of you as "the inconvenient hero."[13] He understood your fleshed-out humanity competed with your performance as a religious person. This is what made you iconic. You aimed to do right. It is righteousness that keeps democracy alive. He saw you close up, pressing into Memphis testifying to the supremacy of love over hate and choosing deliberate protest over complacency, defeat, and resentment. These were your drum major instincts.

Mahalia Jackson understood those instincts too. Her voice gave comfort to yours. No doubt you heard her singing "Move On Up a Little Higher" as you transitioned out of consciousness on the Lorraine Motel's balcony:

> One of these mornings
> Soon one morning
> I'm gonna lay down my cross
> Get me a crown.[14]

6

THE STRENGTH TO LOVE

In the name of love
What more in the name of love
In the name of love
What more in the name of love
—U2, "Pride (In the Name of Love)"[1]

Martin,

Mobilizing in the name of love is quixotic. Envy and shame are the enemies of compassion, and as the political philosopher Martha Nussbaum has observed, they combine to fuel hatred.[2] And hatred is arguably the greatest mobilizer. Factual and alleged grievances, along with the fear of change to the status quo, are easily whipped up in reactionary violent extermination—from Bosnia to Rwanda, where laws, mass execution, and rape were used to ethnically cleanse their respective societies, to the past lynchings and pogroms that have taken place in the United States. Scapegoating an enemy is easier than loving them. Spain's fifteenth-century monarchal merger, the marriage of Isabella and Ferdinand, consolidated the political might of their two kingdoms.

To cement their united throne, they encouraged Pope Paul III to commence the Spanish Inquisition with the task of keeping the new kingdom true blue in its Catholicism. The inquisition thus rooted out the "impure": Jews, Muslims, and shades in between. This vile scapegoating was transnationally endorsed from Europe through the Americas.

There are all kinds of ironies here. The one we must take note of is that you, a Black Baptist preacher, whose namesake, Martin Luther, was one of those virulent anti-Semites influenced by the Inquisition, called for Protestants, Catholics, Jews, and Muslims to ally and mobilize love over hate, historical division, resentment, and stigma. "Let freedom ring," you preached. In your mind it was the democratic quest for freedoms that "will be able to speed up that day when all of God's children, black men and white men, Jews and Gentiles, Protestants and Catholics, will be able to join hands and sing in the words of the old Negro spiritual: *Free at last!*"[3] The kind of love you preached was a different kind of power politics.

I do not know whether it was you or your book marketers at Harper & Row who came up with the title *Strength to Love* for your sermon collection. Whoever it was, I am grateful for this title that conveys love not as sentimental but as a form of spiritual toughness. Marshaling love requires an assemblage as disciplined as a military unit. In other words, love is a force, a potent political force. Throughout your sermons, you distinguished that love was not mushy affect. Love, in your estimation, is a deep and abiding commitment to life itself. It includes *eros* and *philos*, but it is more. It moves beyond sensual attraction and national loyalties. In your theorizing, love is the principled mandate that guides political actions. It is a measured negotiation whose ultimate goal is the respect of personhood. This kind of self-awareness comes from the deepest self-love and self-regard, the biblical injunction to love one's neighbor as oneself. This love requires an ongoing social activism to address the perennial questions of social inequities and the relentless challenges of finitude. A love that acknowledges that ultimately all of us live and die and mandates that, in the between days, daily care be shown to one another.

Your theological ethics generously borrowed from Mohandas Gandhi's satyagraha. Though Gandhi's own bigotries ran deep, his political imagination fueled yours. For Gandhi truth in action was a force for social change. He believed that being truthfully insistent could bring British colonialism to its knees without the debilitations of war. This nonviolent approach would allow all Indians—Hindus, Muslims, Dalits, and others—to build a self-governing nation. Though Gandhi strenuously practiced satyagraha, we know historically that among the diverse people of India this practice was not remotely a reality. Nevertheless, Gandhi's remarkable leadership, even with its limitations, left India intact. He pushed the ball forward. Satyagraha resonated. As a Baptist you understood that many of your people were steeped in biblical lore. They were indoctrinated by the Apostle Paul's idea of love as well as the Hebrew prophets' call for the year of Jubilee. Your version of satyagraha became an adamant and powerful political organizing principle. This required a faith commitment to living justly with one another. A faith that each one of us deserves love was the chief fuel of your ecumenical politics.

Malcolm X, your relentless critic, thought your approach made Black people defenseless. He believed your faith language disempowered, that the Christian gospel defanged Black America and made it less aggressive in demanding human rights. Christian love-talk, he contended with a Nietzschean logic, places the onus on Black folk to be more than human. The expectation that Black folk be more sacrificial is too much to ask. Why should we love when others openly hate us? Why should we show restraint when others can spit on children going to school, blow up and murder those in our houses of worship, and constantly attack our physical well-being with impunity. Had not Black America been the country's sacrificial lambs ten times over, and the Indigenous nations forcibly trapped within the boundaries of the United States more so?

Saint Anselm of Canterbury, an Italian who made his theological career in medieval England, believed that Jesus was the god-man, God's perfect sacrificial substitute for the sins of humanity. In an era filled with constant warfare and the rotting stench of decaying flesh, Anselm reasoned that the sovereign God was akin to a great monarch who held his subjects accountable for their rebelliousness. However, if God were to truly do so, he must wipe humanity from the face of the earth. In the Byzantine logic of the Trinitarian theology, the only loving alternative to mass destruction was as in the biblical narrative of Abraham, who found a ram behind the bush when he proposed to sacrifice Isaac to appease God. Jesus intervened in human history as a sacrificial lamb. He would be substituted on the pyre of human immiseration. "Jesus paid it all, all to him I owe, Sin had left a crimson stain, he washed it white as snow," so goes the hymn we learned.[4]

In an era of terror, Anselm attempted to convey grace, hope, forgiveness, and an ultimately loving God. His reasoning became the conventional wisdom of Rome, promoted by the popularity of the arresting iconography of the sacrificial Jesus carved and painted in cathedrals, chapels, and throne rooms. Royal rationalization did not point to the Galilean peasant struggle that the Romans and King Herod feared. Instead, the narrative was that Jesus paid it all, and we could passively wait from him to return. Anselm's theology, in the fashionable grandeur of baroque art and architecture, allowed enslaving empires to continue to justify their violent colonialism.

But within these empires, it was tens of millions being sacrificed, not just one. For those caught in the web of brutalities—domination, colonialization, enslavement, enclosure, and other forms of human trafficking—Anselm's theology seems to require too much denial. The difficulty with his logic is not a question of sacrifice. Sacrifices can be purposeful. Many sacrifice something for a nobler end: parents go without to provide for children, people forgo their personal finances to support the building of institutions, and soldiers give their lives in war for their comrades. These are not passive acts. The countless persons who are unintentionally caught up in the machinations of avarice, warfare, and systems beyond their individual control are not making self-conscious sacrifices. Their conditions are not normal—as in routine human sufferings. This is why you refashioned Anselm's argumentation. At the Holt Street Baptist Church, you preached that democratic protest in the face of suffering is what the Jewish Jesus taught. You told your people in Montgomery, "If we are wrong, God almighty is wrong."[5]

You knew the history, with all its other interwoven cruelties, of how our enslaved ancestors were repeatedly sacrificed on the brutal altar of a rising capitalist order. Despite two hundred and fifty years of the bullwhip's punishing sting attempting to discipline the souls of Black folk, it proved less than effective. If, as W. E. B. Du Bois observed, White working classes were psychologically paid by the wages of Whiteness, then Black Americans were paid in feelings of powerlessness.[6] Here is a twist in history. Dialogically, in Black Christian communities, Anselm's atoning theology became foundational in rethinking radical self-love. If Jesus paid it all, Black folk could love themselves. In Toni Morrison's *Beloved*, Baby Suggs, a woman preacher and spiritual guide, offers this type of self-radicalism when she gathers her community of battered and maltreated together in a field, urging them to love their broken bodies.

The houses of worship that Black people created for themselves were imperfect temples of self-love. All those houses and spaces of worship, latticed around cities and country towns of the United States, led by all the Baby Suggses, were spaces of otherworldly collective power. "You should love the Lord your God with all your heart, with all your soul, and mind. . . . And a second is like it: 'You should love your neighbor as yourself.'"[7] It was Black folk who memorized this Gospel passage as mantra. You told them that political struggle required the strength to love. You asked them to find an inner potency and demonstrate selfless love within the body politic—an atoning love. This you believed was not weakness but power, and it was derived not from hate but from those who loved us.

Your critics charged that your call to love in political struggle was irrelevant. What Black folk needed, they argued, were expressions of ethnic chauvinism, a self-love rooted in a political power as pernicious as those who sacrificed Black folk on the altars of fear and greed.[8] They overstated the case as perhaps you understated yours. Self-love is more than chic aesthetics and political radicalism without membership in a political party. Collective power takes many forms. In your mind, engaging in civil disobedience was a demonstration of Black collective self-love. We love ourselves by challenging structures of capital and law that made Black folk less than human. Self-love is radically manifested through protest with the goal of expanding democratic inclusivity. Democracy is not just for a select elite; it must be deliberately challenged to include the Black, the Brown, the Indigenous, the Asian, the White, and all those in between. To build the people's power, you required their participation. Your Southern Nonviolent Coordinating Committee (SNCC) comrades did this better than you or the SCLC, the latter being so steeped in sexist preacherly hierarchy. Nevertheless, you learned.

All efforts to achieve an end require sacrifice, perhaps those making social change more so. Whether one agrees with Anselm's medieval formulation of Jesus as a paid ransom to Satan, one cannot disagree that Jesus and so many others sacrificed themselves in struggles beyond themselves. And this is where the strength to love is best exhibited. There is an American trope, derivative of ole Ben Franklin's maxim, that one must sacrifice in order to work one's way up monetarily. This faith in one's own self-reliance emphasized individual determination. Your politics of love, however, called for us to cast individualism aside; it ironically resonated more with John Winthrop's "city upon a hill," his covenant aboard the *Arabella* in 1630. Winthrop's notion was that a covenant was not solely about an individual, but a commonwealth of sorts—a people yoked together freely. Your covenant was much larger than his and was not limited to English dissenters. Covenants brokered in other traditions and tongues were being broken while Winthrop's biblically inspired one settled into the Massachusetts Bay Colony.

Admittedly, Winthrop's model of a covenant, the idea that God entered a contract with a particular people for good, has a less-than-noble past. The Puritan massacre of the Pequot in Connecticut in 1637 devolved into the total subjugation of various Indigenous people of the region, and this perverse history was echoed globally. Americo-Liberians, though not fully successful, sought to dominate the Indigenous people of Liberia—the Grebo, the Kpelle, the Kru, and the Vai. Joseph Smith, Brigham Young, and their successors in Utah terrorized Indigenous people too, even though the Book of Mormon sacralized Native peoples. The South African Boers, the Dutch-speaking immigrants who trekked east to escape British dominance, claimed Ndebele lands in the name of the Boer God. And the Israelis, who have a history of dogged oppression and suffering throughout Europe, are turned into political weapons to disfranchise and expel their Arab-speaking neighbors, akin to the US South's Lost Cause, the myth that the South was heroic and wronged by Union troops during the Civil War.

The framers of the Constitution could not have imagined back in the late eighteenth century the Black people you mobilized, whose ancestors were simply the chattel hidden in the spaces and nuanced silences of the original wording of the Constitution. You were part of the birth of a new order.

As a seminarian you had begun to think about the meaning of a new democratic covenant as you examined the book of Jeremiah. You described the book as having a spiritual tension between ritual legalities and spiritual aims of the law.

> The children of the New Covenant would be the sons of God, no longer subject to external laws of the state, but ruled by impulses to good, acting upon the heart as a principle which grows from within.[9]

Channeling Howard Thurman, you argued this covenant was born of a spiritual journey. Your own inward journey brought you to the recognition that it was Black Americans who paid the heaviest cost for demanding a more ecumenical freedom for all. You knew that politicians and their corporate allies thought they could cheaply fix society's racism. They offered what Dietrich Bonhoeffer, the German theologian who opposed the Nazi Party, called "cheap grace."[10] Or as you stated, "it didn't cost the nation anything to desegregate lunch counters."[11] But there are no cheap reconciliations or resolutions. It is costly to repair structural flaws in a building, as it is in a society. Truthfully, there is a stiff payment at the human rights toll both to be paid. Countless named and unnamed pay that cost. You knew going into battle that this would be the case; you were a student of history. The babies, the young, the volunteers, and the fellow movement leaders whom you buried were incalculably crushing to the spirit. This is why you preached the strength to love.

Active love is spiritual warfare, as apocalyptically portrayed in the book of Ephesians. Hatred is always the undertow of societies. It can quickly drown movements, nations, and people in irrationality and violence—the Tulsa Massacre, Kigali's slaughter, the Nuremberg Rallies, Phnom Penh's Killing Fields, and the Srebrenica genocide. Hate is such a strong intoxicant that it severely impairs the moral imagination. It is the deadliest of wet dreams. So, it takes strength to remain abstemious from murderous ends. Collectively, people binging on hate stampede like the bulls of Pamplona. When the hangover commences, the only thing left are excuses: "It was not our fault" or "We were not at the scene of the crime." But truth has a way of finding us all out.

Too often younger writers and scholars—whether Ta-Nehisi Coates or the bevy of Black Power historians—too quickly elide this dimension of struggle when looking back upon the 1960s. Active love was a way of disciplining a movement. It was also about shaking off the internalized feelings of unworthiness lodged in the psyche of Black communities. Reviewing films, novels, and plays—including Amiri Baraka's 1964 *Dutchman*, Charles Burnett's 1990 *To Sleep with Anger*, Charles Fuller's 1981 *A Soldier's Play*, Adrienne Kennedy's 1964 *Funnyhouse of a Negro*, Toni Morrison's 1970 *The Bluest Eye*—testifies to how internalized self-hatred can be. This movement was just as much about being democratic to ourselves as it was about showing forgiveness to White perpetrators of racial violence. It takes strength to love ourselves, just as much strength as it requires to "love some of our sick white brothers,"[12] as you cleverly phrased your outrage at White terrorism.[13]

In your mind, we practice self-love by engaging in confrontational democratic politics.

Loving politics (like the name of the United States Supreme Court case *Loving v. Virginia*, which you lived to see) is about self-liberation. However, this politics cannot be reduced to a form of political correctness. Loving politics is all about democracy and legalities, the laws conferred to protect each of us. It was part of your new democratic covenant assuring that each of us must be protected from hateful scorn, whether due to our age, (dis)abilities, language, race, sexualities, social class, or combination thereof. The covenant behind your politics was muscular love, not hate.

In 1999 law professor and novelist Stephen Carter argued in his book *Civility* that democracies require sacrifice.[14] To build for the common good, democracy requires that each of us extend mutuality, respect, and courtesy to our fellow citizens. Carter's idea is not that we do not have disagreements; he does not propose for us to become simplistically nice, with smiling faces. Rather, he argues that civility is a requirement of a democracy. We must abide the rules of respectful engagement, like the US Senate's courteous address of "my fellow Senator." We must announce our agreement that we are members of a common body before launching into our disagreements. Announcing that we belong to a common body is our first act of civility. The rules of civility and civic engagement require us to sacrifice self-centeredness to assure dialogue and cooperation. This was true as you and your fellow activists warred on the battlefield of human rights. You understood the common fight but addressed one another respectfully as you disagreed. The internal politics of the movement modeled how neighborly love fostered the good society. "The true genius of Martin Luther King, Jr." Carter penned, "was not in his ability to articulate the pain of an oppressed people—many other preachers did so, with as much passion and as much power—but in his ability to inspire those very people to be loving and civil in their dissent." And there is nothing particularly objectionable about what he offers regarding your intent. "The civil rights movement wanted to expand American democracy, not destroy it, and he understood that uncivil dialogue serves no democratic function. Democracy demands dialogue, and dialogue flows from disagreement."

There is much to appreciate about Carter's assessment. He's right that civility is a form of democratic sacrifice for the common good. However, his read of the civil rights movement is idealized. The frustration that many of your critics felt resulted from the accumulation of sacrifices. We always bore them. In every war the country fought, Black folk participated with valor, but rarely was that patriotism honored with common respect. Black World War II veterans returned to the South threatened, intimidated, and murdered with impunity. Civil rights workers and volunteers were routinely threatened and frequently murdered. In both the North and the South, police brutality continued unabated long before Black Lives Matter. By 1966 many civil rights activists were exhausted and traumatized by the level of mayhem that was used against them just for integrating a lunch counter, riding a bus, or moving into a non-Black community. The murderous harassment was constant. And this is one of the problems with Carter's argument: he never acknowledges the sacrifices that Black Americans have made collectively to alter American democracy.

The political philosopher Danielle Allen argues in a similar vein as Carter. For her, democracy is renewed through the sacrifice of maintaining political friendships.[15] Friendship requires us to give one another the benefit of the doubt and make room that we could be wrong in our opinions. I agree to some extent, but her analogy can only go so far. We have relationships to enemies just as much as to our friends. We can healthily respect those we oppose with all our might. Of course, we must give each other space to make mistakes without throwing the entirety of a relation-ship out the window. However, we must acknowledge, just as you did, that in loving our enemies we see that those we direly oppose have humanity. It is political wisdom to recognize the realities of enemies. Your radicalism called for us to love our enemies—not necessarily be their friends. This is not unmanneredly. Allen does not make this distinction as clearly as she might have. Enemies are brought warily to the table for a common end, not friendship.

Bringing warring parties to the table in civil negotiation is the beginning of wisdom. This is the beginning of love in action. It is not romance but a practical recognition that détente must eventually be arrived at. Peace thus comes out of that recogni-tion. Recognition, though, is not enough. As the philosopher Georg Wilhelm Hegel understood, the slave owner recognizes the slave—the question is just what kind of recognition is it to be seen as fully human? Here Carter might have taken the more pessimistic thought of theologian Jean Calvin more seriously. Human beings, Calvin argued, are prone to delude themselves that they are the totality of the universe—in other words, God.

This is the quest of imperial rule. Imperialism leads nations and leaders to forget that their collective acts of malfeasance are built on the backs of people. Calvin believed each of us, from creation, has an inborn will to power, what the nineteenth-century phi-losopher Friedrich Nietzsche viewed as the drive that all human beings are born possessing. It is only when people attempt to impose their values on others that the will to power becomes dangerous. Calvin was far more pessimistic than Nietzsche. Will to power is the will to be god-like, which was delusional in his estimation. This is the human condition, and it must be con-stantly checked and reformed. Depravity does not simply arise from bad individual moral choices; it is a collective activity that fosters estrangement from the divine and alienates us from our neighbors. Calvin's pessimism is disliked by many, but there is a great deal of truth in his understanding of power and its use for all sorts of inhumane crimes, even his own. In Calvin's mind, humanity is always in a constant struggle to limit selfish pride. So as much as Carter calls on us to sacrifice for our neighbor, it may result in more harm because of human greed and pride, to take the theological approach of Calvin. Black Americans have historically been civil, imposing codes of respectability upon themselves. Civility, however, is often a cloak of the powerful to criticize and subdue righteous uprisings. Civility is not conferred to all without a forceful response to reduce the powerfully entrenched, who impose their values without regard to the well-being of others.

You recognized the depth of these internal and external political realities. It was always your hope that, though we must struggle against injustices, we keep our humanity. We must always recognize the humanity of our enemies. They, too, you believed, are children of God. This was how you defined your political radicalness: by the measure of how much you could love yourself as well as your adversaries.

But this is difficult because entrenched power is unrelenting. The reality is our adversaries use sophisticated media to gin up hatred. Lynchings were promoted by newspapers. Advertising agencies develop focus groups to foment anxious fears. Radio is used to spew propaganda. And new social mediums source untruths. The truth is that there are powerful enemies who refuse to share power and do almost anything not to share it. You idealistically asked us to have a higher humanity.

Our fight for democracy has been historically tortuous, and it has left us filled with self-doubt and self-blame to a criminal degree. How can neighborly love be manifested if we do not truly love ourselves as a people? This has been a ceaseless question in all our freedom struggles. However noble Black American histories are, we have grappled with three hundred years of psychological and material deprivations. Whatever the past has meant to any one of us, we must acknowledge that strangulation has been a constant theme. Eric Garner, the Black New Yorker who was strangled to death by police officers on video gasping plaintively, "I can't breathe," sums up this dimension of our histories succinctly.

It is the story of the pregnant field hand who works up until the moment her water breaks. It is the story at the auction block of a knee-high offspring cavalierly thrown into a deal for good measure. It is the learned, self-regulating color coding: "if you are yellow, you are mellow; if you're Brown, stick around; if you're Black, get back." It is the harsh sentencing for selling a bag of weed. All of these and more are the ghosts at our dining room tables. This accumulative history haunted you too. You desperately feared being late for class at Crozer Theological Seminary, dreading your White classmates would see you as an imaginary shiftless Black worker. You too were "color struck," dating only young women no darker than the shade of a tan paper bag. You, like the rest of us, wrestled with the self-abasement that oppression inflicts. Our troublesome guest who's coming to dinner has always been self-loathing. Your critics wanted you to preach about more self-love than self-sacrificial love.

What your critics seem to have forgotten was that Black self-love *is* a self-sacrificing love. All of the institutions that Black people struggled to build—their businesses, churches, clubs, colleges, mosques, schoolhouses, and temples—required sacrifice. No, they did not rival some of their wealthy counterparts in materiality, but they belonged to us. Truth is: Black people have always exercised power, even when it was most limited and under surveillance. You took for granted that your children's generation understood their parents' and grandparents' self-sacrifice as a form of love for their communities. Instead of seeing self-love in action, too many young people only learned of struggle as negative. It was to be escaped rather than embraced. However, what you wanted them to see was that life itself is a struggle that must be guided by an ethic. For you the mobilization of love was a political act that clarified our own self-regard in our efforts to create a more transparent democracy.

Fast-forward. In 1995 Minister Louis Farrakhan made a powerful call for Black men to come to Washington, DC, on behalf of their brothers, children, wives, and women, as though chivalry would save our communities from the steady erosion of benefit-paying factory jobs that rewarded brawn and punctuality. In his Million Man March, Farrakhan called millions of Black men to make the journey to DC, following the lead of Bayard Rustin, an openly gay Black man and the ingenious logistician of the March on Washington. Farrakhan understood the desperation of the moment and called men to come to the nation's capital.

But Farrakhan lacked a policy agenda. Black men were to love themselves without a mobilizing strategy that involved their aunts, daughters, friends, lovers, mothers, and sisters. This strategy, politically vacuous as it was, did not take into consideration that the people who walked the halls of Congress were coconspirators in the demise of civility within Black communities. The root of Black lovelessness and of the deterioration of communal virtue was political and capital divestment. Farrakhan's ebony Promise Keepers gathering, though noble in intent, was a political failure.

In contrast, the massive protests you led in DC demanded policy changes. The Prayer Pilgrimage for Freedom commemorated the US Supreme Court ruling in *Brown v. Board of Education* and demanded the Civil Rights Act of 1957 be bolstered with voting rights. On that stage, you so deftly sermonized the nation with "Give Us the Ballot."[16] Six years later, at the 1963 March on Washington, your "I Have a Dream" speech pushed for better employment opportunity and again called for a civil rights act stronger than the one enacted in 1957.

Minister Farrakhan's 1995 summoning of Black men to Washington, DC, should have been a call for democratic change. Although the Million Man March exceeded the March on Washington numerically, Farrakhan's emphasis on changing male personal behavior without making concrete demands on the body politic was a missed opportunity. Perhaps he should have called for Congress to repeal the 1994 Violent Crime Control and Law Enforcement Act, a bill that unduly punished the million men he called together.[17] His call for atonement ironically encouraged more Black blame. Instead of seeking responsible justice, he unintentionally placed the burden on Black men to behave as bourgeois patriarchs without the capitalist underpinnings. Farrakhan's call was affirmative, but without social strategies, this kind of self-love was limited.

The struggle to love oneself and one's neighbor is the most challenging thing that any of us can do. It requires so much deliberate intent and self-awareness. This is why you advocated that political struggle be carried out prayerfully. This prayerfulness or mindfulness need not be pious recognition of a benevolent God. It can be offered as our very best hope for a just universe. Your prayer for strength came out of a belief that if Jesus could withstand the cross while acting in the name of a loving God, you could withstand American scornfulness in a struggle for an inclusive democracy.

Prayers have various motivations. However, the very best of them seek strength to persevere despite heartache and setbacks. Prayer is about the strength to carry on. True prayer is not self-deception. It is the recognition that having an optimistic mindset will not necessarily change our difficult circumstances. The strength to love allows us to face the hungry lions within the Colosseum. It is the mindfulness necessary to endure negative attacks while pushing a righteous agenda. It is our pliant request to subdue our egos for a greater good.

In the end, the strength to love is a self-offering for a greater cause. You called us to interject Black communal self-love found in our own community institutions. This love, you believed, is the beginning effort in a greater struggle against selfish capital, group adulation, and racist chauvinism. The strength to love beckons us to formulate a new covenant, one that supersedes inequitable legalities and managerial bigotries. The strength to love is a constant struggle to negotiate and renegotiate the terms of civic community. You believed that love is an oppositional power, one that we should powerfully exercise in making democratic change. Either we live together as siblings in a community, you warned, or we die together as fools.

7

WE AS A PEOPLE

If you're ready
If you're ready now
If you're ready, yeah
Come on go with me
—Staple Singers,
"If You're Ready (Come Go with Me)"[1]

Martin,

You went to Memphis to lend support to striking sanitation work-ers for what we call today a "living wage." Your presence and pres-tige accorded their strike international significance. So, everyone attending Mason Temple Church of God in Christ that rainy night knew exactly what you meant when you crescendoed, "I may not get there with you, but . . . we as a people will get to the promised land!"[2] They were bowled over! That was a radical ending on the night of April 3, 1968. Though you spoke forebodingly, like you had done before, no one could have fully imagined that your life would come to an end twenty-four hours later. That denouement was outstanding. Yet it has always left me wondering just what you meant by "we as a people." Did you mean, as I heard it, that Black folk were going to get to the promised land? Or did you mean all US citizens?

Professor Eddie Glaude's book *Exodus!: Religion, Race, and Nation in Early Nineteenth-Century Black America* explores this trajectory of Black political consciousness. Philosophically, he brings to light that Black Americans have had a long history of "we-ness." Glaude's study of political solidarity begins with the mid-nineteenth-century Colored Convention Movement, a small national organization struggling to come together to dethrone slavery.[3] Inspired by philosophical pragmatism, he studied the political ideology of Black people from the perspective of whether or not it practically worked for Black communities in the nineteenth century. Glaude's book traces how the competing sense of peoplehood that was imaginatively derived from the Torah and the New Testament has been foundational to the politics of Black liberation. Black folk, like the ancient Hebrews, have sojourned through varying oppressive conditions—enslavement, exile, loss of sovereignty, nation building, and unfaithful leadership. Ethiopianism, which existed before the Colored Convention Movement, holds that Africa has a biblical history, and enslavement is not a fait accompli for those enslaved or those living on the African continent.

Religious historian Albert Raboteau describes Ethiopianism as a form of theodicy, a way of ennobling the mass sufferings and deaths of those enslaved in North America and the Caribbean. Joseph, the dreamer—having been sold into Egypt by his jealous brothers, only to become the king's chief minister and the eventual savior of his people—was the defining symbol of what those enslaved in the US were to become for African people. The end of Black suffering was the salvation of African people.[4] Glaude argues that Black folk who lived in North America and the Anglophone Caribbean creatively grafted onto religious narratives to describe their conditions. Whether one agrees with this assessment or not, the roots of Black political consciousness are found in the language of the King James Bible; if that bible shaped English nationalism, it was equally formative in giving Black Americans a unifying sense of peoplehood.

From slavery to emancipation, the sense of peoplehood has been diversified by social class, religious orientation, and region. We-ness has always been prismatic. Today, Black political scientists as diverse as Michael C. Dawson and Melanye T. Price have used data sets, focus groups, and political theorizing to discuss the pros and cons of what this we-ness means in today's politics.[5] They identify that there are conflicting streams of we-ness. This collective identity has to some extent carried the seeds of xenophobia, even before recent political protests of the American Descendants of Slavery (ADOS).

In spite of these stratifications, there is a collective affinity, a sense of peoplehood, an imperfect collective awareness born of struggle. That peoplehood was shaped by democratic institutions internal to black communities. Solidarity, according to the philosopher Tommy Shelby in *We Who Are Dark: The Philosophical Foundations of Black Solidarity*, continues to be unevenly manifested in Black communities.[6] And journalist Eugene Robinson, in his anxiety-filled *Disintegration: The Splintering of Black America*, has written of its alarming dissipation.[7] All these writers acknowledge a we-ness, but they all miss a central part of it. This we-ness has been persistently cultivated by a spirituality rooted in Black Protestantism. Whether they believe it or not, we-ness was cultivated by a spirituality, an ethos that Du Bois attempted to define as "souls."

Too often the glue of the spirit is overlooked. Peoplehood must have an adhesive, a coagulant, whether secular or religious. Journalists and scholars fail to see what you learned from your father and the preachers that surrounded you. They understood how to keep their fold together and create a vision for them to build together. Weekly, you informed the people at the church on Dexter and Auburn Avenues of their common destiny, encouraging them to work together and cherish one another in spite of any personal enmities. In your sermons, we-ness was no abstract concept. It was the persistent effort to keep a cooperative unity and build community. If a preacher cannot get her folk to work together, her church will not function as an organization for spiritual well-being. Her calling is to define what it means to be a people. Being a people is not a given. It requires cultivation, intentionality, and ritual.

And here lies the irritation. Politically and culturally, the United States prioritizes the individual. Liberal democracy is theoretically based on individuals, not collectives. The premise is one person, one vote. Liberalism can also protect the accumulated assets of an individual against royal economic monopoly. The irony here is that those assets were often gained through a royal monopoly or decree. In theory, the state ought not be able to take an individual's property without strong justification that it is in the interest of the overall good. The rights of the person are more sacrosanct than the rights of communities. Democratic processes are designed to protect the person, and communal rights are seemingly in conflict with individuality.

Individuality is so much a part of US culture that we assume it is the natural order of things. Jazz that arose out of Black communities put great emphasis on individual voicing, uniqueness of sound and style. This musical culture was one of writer Ralph Ellison's greatest influences. This explains in part the emphasis on individuality in his novel *Invisible Man*. The narrator looks to define himself in a Harlem where others impose a collective identity upon him. The problem for the narrator, like it is for all of us, is that we negotiate ourselves in relationship to other selves. Ellison, however, was smitten with individual virtuosity, and I understand this as coming out of his musical sensibility.

In jazz, voicing must always be truthful. It is a requirement of the blues aesthetic to be intellectually honest when one steps up to solo. The beauty of the music allows for self-expression even in a group. That individuality expressed through a virtuoso's performance enhances the group performance and the overall body of the song, but the soloist could never replace the band. There are limits to being a soloist. The narrator of *Invisible Man*, in his stadium-lit underground chamber, may vividly contemplate his self-understanding, but that individuality is no substitute for collective social engagement. Whether playing in a band, participating in a political organization, or being a member of a team, there is always a limit to individual virtuosity.

Human beings are not only individuals. Democracy protects our individuality, as it should, but it cannot spare us from negotiating with a collective. No matter how many lights we have shining upon us, our individuality must come into some negotiation with our fellow human beings. Collectivity must always have limits placed upon it too, lest one is suffocated by groupthink. Within a collective, room must be given for self-expression. Ellison's great fear, and rightfully so, is that the collective will suffocate our individuality. This is precisely how the narrator feels. So peoplehood must always be balanced by a rejection of stale and hackneyed essentialism. Folk must be free to question unifying themes when they do not allow us to breathe. This is why jazz is considered to be democratic: it heterophonically interweaves self-expression to create group expression.

I love that Ellison emphasizes individual self-expression; it is perfectly Emersonian. Like his namesake, Ralph Waldo Emerson, who sought in the nineteenth century to reformulate his own burdensome Puritan heritage, Ellison challenged Black societal sameness. The rich variety of Black persons have never been formulaic in our effort to live dignified lives. We are alive in all our aspirations and contradictions. However personally rewarding Ellison's novel has been for me, it is as politically flawed as Emerson's notion of self-reliance. The senior Ralph Waldo attempted to shed a personal history steeped in a collective religious compact and substitute it with a freeing individuality. "There is a time in every man's education when he arrives at the conviction that envy is ignorance; that imitation is suicide; that he must take himself for better, for worse, as his portion; that though the wide universe is full of good, no kernel of nourishing corn can come to him but through his toil bestowed on that plot of ground which is given to him to till."[8] Unwittingly this played into well-established patterns of greed and political dominion. Agrarian chiefs, captains of industry, and ruthless entrepreneurs would come to excuse their factory manipulation and exploitation of human capital as an expression of their individual creative power. They envisioned themselves as the self-reliant.

However, Ellison's narrator, like countless unseen persons, also needs a collective body to hang his personal freedoms on. Hanging out in a voluminous, lit sanctum by oneself will never by itself bring reconciliation to the antidemocratic elements in US history. At its best, democracy is a balance between our individual desires and the collective good. This is true for any freedom struggle.

Puritans were British subjects tagged by their seventeenth-century critics for seeking a life of pure biblical Christianity. They sought to escape England and build community as though they were ancient Hebrews. Six decades ago the historian Perry Miller richly described Puritan preachments in *Errand into the Wilderness*. They were sojourners, volunteer participants who followed their God into the North American wilderness. The irony is that that this wilderness was filled with people, just as the Hebrew wilderness was filled with Canaanites. Puritans found themselves in a land populated by the Iroquois, Lenape, Massachusett, and

Pequot. The Puritan religiopolitical utopia came into conflict with the faiths, dreams, and traditions of preexisting communities. Ultimately, hardened Puritans, veterans from Europe's religious wars, would view these Indigenous peoples as their Canaanites to be conquered. This way of knowing would repeat itself around the globe as the Voortrekkers, Dutch-speaking settlers in South Africa attempting to escape British domination in the South African Cape Colony, marched militarily into the Transvaal region, ultimately at the expense of Zulus. Contemporaneously with the Voortrekkers, Mormons, members of the Church of Jesus Christ of Latter-Day Saints, fled their religious oppression and trekked across US states and territories, only to inflict oppression on the Numa, Shoshone, and Ute. This, too, was justified by their religious nationalism. What is problematic about these historical narratives is that they were used to other. Toni Morrison described this as "otherness," or in your words, "thingification."[9] Otherness as a narrative of nationalism is used to create hierarchical order by excluding narratives of those deemed "other."

Generations of US historians enshrined Puritan logic as the sum of our national history. What is called "American exceptionalism" was supposedly born upon the *Arabella*, the ship where John Winthrop, the Puritan governor and spiritual muse of the Massachusetts Bay Colony, exhorted his fellow congregants to be a new people—a global representation of Christian charity. The US narrative was told in your day as though it had no Indigenous peoples or Roman Catholics, let alone Africans! These historians spilled a great deal of nationalist ink debating the hows and whys of the framers, the Declaration of Independence, and the United States Constitution. In the main, these were not fully objective analyses of the early republic but rather hagiographies of the White male elite, which many of the historians themselves were. I am not saying these histories had nothing to teach us regarding the law, popular sovereignty, and other matters emerging in the United States. However, histories without underlying transnational commercialism and that exclude the people who worked the land are suspect, then and now.

These White upper-class histories, like the country itself, have been constantly challenged since the country's formation. Black historians have repudiated the cultural chauvinism embedded in White writings on US history. They have been autobiographically rendered, fleshed out in scolding jeremiads, reasoned with dispassionate lectures, and vividly sermonized. There has always been this other "we the people." White historical omissions were not accidental. Those who wish to maintain power constantly defined and refabricated innocence. They did not wish to acknowledge that Anglo-nationalism is buttressed by sexist racism, and thus, they can never be fully honest. Behind the names of Adams, Franklin, Jefferson, and Madison were the daily lives of unnamed children, men, and women who toiled without political or economic inclusion.

Scholar Saidiya Hartman's penetrating analysis of the Constitution and the Federalist Papers in *Scenes of Subjection: Terror, Slavery, and Self-Making in Nineteenth-Century America* reminds us that as noble as some of their sentiments are, these documents are also tools of dominion. In various scenarios across the nineteenth century, subjugation has been disguised as freedom. Freedom via Constitutional interpretation was narrowed to support the interests of the few—not the enslaved, not the poor and landless, and not indigenous nations expelled from their lands. Hartman's analysis strips off the varnish of Constitutional grandiosity to reveal how power is used to suppress a fuller democracy. Today the Federalist Society, an organization of conservative lawyers acting as the supposed guardians of the Federalist Papers, protects the legal doctrine of "original intent." This "originalism" was born from the forehead of the late Justice Antonin Scalia, like Athena was birthed from Zeus. It is a clever way of conservatively interpreting the Constitution. For Scalia, this meant that the Constitution's initial public meaning, when it was first enacted into law, determines all future interpretation. Like in the notion of biblical inerrancy that girds Christian fundamentalism, originalism values the printed text over the spirit of the text. The silliness of Justice Scalia's idea is that his fellow conservative Associate Justice Clarence Thomas, along with the Catholics, Jews, and women justices who sit on the Supreme Court today, would not be justices if this were a reality. The original intent of the US Constitution supported the US's White Protestant supremacy as a slaveholding colonial nation. US liberal discourse such as Scalia's continues to be shrouded in a cynical evasion, never admitting openly how this devilish garrulousness legitimizes and maintains political and economic dominance over ordinary citizens seeking to expand democratic freedoms. The individualist language of the constitutional order hides the collective power of wealth and privilege. This liberalism favored the planter—today the corporations that are richer than the poorest nation-state—over the exploited laborer, the landless destitute, and the widow. And this is one of the reasons why we as a country have been in a tumultuous political and intellectual struggle.

All this history was featured in your Memphis finale. That evening, a thunderstorm shook the night sky. It was your final live performance, and it was as stirring as your opening one in Montgomery at the Holt Street Baptist Church. That Memphis audience mirrored your very first one in Montgomery. The audience was made up of high schoolers, janitors, maids, preachers, sanitation workers, schoolteachers, and the plain-old cynically curious. They came to hear your words pour over them like a magical elixir, needing to be strengthened in their struggle for human decency and fairer wages. Your words were alchemy, transmuting their daily indignities into something bigger and larger than they thought imaginable. And you did not disappoint them.

That night you were the consummate revivalist showman. You drew the audience in with a fanciful rhetorical flight across a Eurocentric historical landscape, a theologically informed Western civilization class. The audience was guided through ancient Greece and Rome to the Renaissance and Reformation, where your name-sake, Martin Luther, followed his conscience to resist Roman Catholic orthodoxy in Wittenberg. You told the jubilantly recep-tive audience that you would not even stop at Abraham Lincoln's signing of the Emancipation Proclamation. You finally landed on 1968, when you stood alongside sanitation workers striking in Memphis. It was a masterful oratorical flourish.

In hindsight your soaring speechmaking that rainy evening might have been even better had you explained how 240 years of slave economics was a US inheritance. Memphis is named after the ancient Egyptian imperial capital, a city scaffolded upon the backs of the most brutally efficient slave labor. Slaves in the United States crossed the South's fertile delta, which spanned eleven states. They carried mounds and pounds of material goods to be sold worldwide, commercial futures that depended on the exploitation of their humanity. Intellectually and experi-entially, you knew that slavery shaped everyone seated in that cavernous Church of God in Christ sanctuary. Your audience's forbearers had weathered chattel slavery and pogroms such as the 1866 Memphis "race riot." You were all in a fight to win your own emancipation. The foundations of your listeners' resistance, the very defiance that you were asking them to wage nonvio-lently, had its beginnings in the dank steerage of various middle passages.

Protestantism shaped various African tongues into Black Amer-icanness. The beginnings of our freedom struggles are found in the word, language that resisted the totalizing exploitation. Black suffering and resistance found symbiotic concord with metaphors and similes in the English translation of the Bible. The King James translation of the Bible provided a source of political solidarity just as it had done for seventeenth-century English imperialists. By the 1830s, as conquered Native territories became slave states, there was only the word made flesh to affirm the bondspeople sold "down the river." In the beginning was the word, and it was freedom. Though united by the word, Black folk were never uniform in their expressions of the word. In published narratives and field songs, interpretations of freedom came in different colors. They could all agree that human degradation was not to be tolerated. Even with class colorism creating further division, there was a common belief that human beings should never be kidnapped and exploited till death. If the word condemned anything, it condemned commandeering the bodies and the souls of sentient beings.

In a sermon at Dexter Avenue Baptist Church titled "Unfulfilled Hopes" (eerily given on April 5, 1959, nine years almost to the date before your assassination), you told your members that Black creativity is born in resistance to enslavement. These resistances have taken place everywhere—aboard ships, in rice swamps, in the rows of sugar cane and tobacco, and in towns throughout the slaveholding Americas. After slavery's demise, the efforts to expand democratic freedoms continued, and the stories of these efforts are buried atrocities. They continue to haunt cities like Colfax and Thibodaux in Louisiana, Hamburg and Phoenix in South Carolina, and larger cities across the country. Though squelched and denied widespread publicity, Black resistance has been steadfast. It is the fuel behind our arts, our intellectual inquiries, and our sense of democratic governance. Even when the rebellions are not successful, we have persisted in the word. You preached:

Out of these black men and these black women came
something that keeps the generations going. If they had
turned to the first method of bitterness, it wouldn't have
come. If they had withdrawn and turned to silent hate, it
wouldn't have come. But it came because of the creativity
of the will and the dynamic quality of it, and the determination to stand up, amid all of those forces, amid all
of the darkness of human circumstance.[10]

That stormy night in Memphis, speaking to the striking sanitation workers at Mason Temple, you improvised. You summoned
enough hope to convince everyone, even yourself, that the struggle
was worthwhile. The weariness in your eyes said it all. You intoned
like bluesman Robert Johnson. A hellhound was on your trail:

I got to keep movin', I got to keep movin'
Blues fallin' down like hail, blues fallin' down like hail
And the days keeps on worryin' me
There's a hellhound on my trail, hellhound on my trail[11]

You once more acknowledged that death was impending.
Then came your fearless crescendo, analogous to Moses seeing
the promised land. It was the showstopper. The sanctuary erupted!
The audience received your spellbinding oration with thunderous
applause. You courageously stood with them. These people were
going to the promised land.

Promised lands, however, are tricky. All too often being a people destined for a promised land has meant being over against
another set of people. Utopian dreams of a promised land frequently begin with murderous eruptions and repressed traumas.
They send people who have spiritual solidarity on a journey, but
sadly, it is not a shared journey for everyone. One group's political

dominance is another's metaphorical Egypt. Toni Morrison's novel *Paradise*, situated in the imagined all-Black territory—reminiscent of the all-Black towns in Oklahoma—reminds us that, more specifically, one group's paradise can be a living hell filled with murderous misogyny for Black women. So the promised land analogy is limited. You never dreamt, I am sure, of enacting violent conquest in order to unify a Black promised land. The promised land you urged did not come from brutalizing others. Your envisioned promised land was a fully democratized country. You believed that what makes Black Americans a world-historical people is a collective vigilance to fight for the sacredness of human personhood. In Montgomery at the beginning of your public career, you pronounced:

> As we stand and sit here this evening and as we prepare ourselves for what lies ahead, let us go out with a grim and bold determination that we are going to stick together. We are going to work together. Right here in Montgomery, when the history books are written in the future somebody will have to say, "There lived a race of people[,] a black people, 'fleecy locks and black complexion,' a people who had the moral courage to stand up for their rights. And thereby they injected a new meaning into the veins of history and of civilization." And we're gonna do that. God grant that we will do it before it is too late. As we proceed with our program let us think of these things.[12]

Those were lofty expectations.

You knew Black politics was limited by self-censoring judgmentalism, arising from the growth of the middle class and poverty's fatalism. Despite these impediments, you saw the key to Black solidarity was a spirituality. Solidarity is not simply transactional; it is the concrete blocks of every democratic institution. In Memphis, the cemetery of pharaohs, you had spiritual solidarity with the audience. You established we-ness with the women and men toiling as the cheapest laborers, overutilized and underpaid. From Montgomery to Memphis, in their houses of prayer and in their daily social interactions, filled with laughter, love, and the teeth-sucking sound of pettiness, they sustained an enduring power to push for justice in the courts and on the streets, even when this spirituality was not evident to the US majority.

It is this persistent strength that continues to remake our democracy today. Black America flipped the script on a racialized democratic state to make it more perfect. It is Black people's fight that makes the United States exceptional. It is our cultural ecumenism that makes our country shine brightly to the world's people. Other peoples see links to Black freedom struggles; this is what makes the Bill of Rights live.

Conservative thinkers and politicians have enjoyed twisting your words. They love lifting a single line in your "I Have Dream" speech. Writer and scholar Michael Eric Dyson is correct that your ideas have been bastardized.[13] Your statement that you wanted your children judged by the "content of their character" as opposed "to the color of their skin" was not an affirmation of radical libertarianism and unbridled capitalism. It was an affirmation of what every true Baptist knows—that is, that every person must give account for what they did for others before the Almighty. The basis of this religious anthropology is fellowship, which brings people together for good. Character, then, is not pomposity of a virtuous self, because no person is ever truly virtuous. The truest dimension of character is how each person stands in relationship to their communities, their loved ones, and the collective needs they see around them.

What conservative thinkers have been oblivious to—in their justification of rampant individualism for greed's sake—is the depth of character derived from Black struggle. Conservatism continues to promote a narrative that a distinct pathology exists among Black folk, as though the social conditions we have faced is a traceable virus. This is a narrative repeated so often that it forced W. E. B. Du Bois in *The Souls of Black Folk* at the turn of the twentieth century to ponder, "How does it feel to be a problem?"[14] Black and White conservatives alike, however, missed your point in Washington entirely. You were discussing the real content of our character: our ability to put on our marching shoes, pick up our intifada stones, and bravely stand before unjust militarized law enforcement. The real content of our character is and has always been our ability to dangerously create—to paraphrase Edwidge Danticat—spaces where we can all breathe.[15] It does not take much character to defend wealthy racist oligarchs. Character comes in organizing "protest for right"![16] Character is political and demands equality! It is the struggle to assure that no human being is a permanent subaltern or caste member, spiritually or politically. The normalization of racist fodder, the pathogen found in the Spanish Inquisition and carried on in European centers, shaped the so-called New World. It was rehashed in subsequent nationalisms and nation-states. This is why the rich and powerful have always found our spiritual dissent politically disconcerting.

This has always made us a dangerous, democratic people. We share affinities with all those facing genocide, unjust incarcerations, impoverishment, low wages, physical terror, and systematic exclusions. Our democratic ideology, derived from our abilities to transcend historical alienations, has always been the source of our political power. This is why so much political energy is spent by our political opposition trying to dismantle our sense of we-ness. Our peoplehood joins human suffering and struggle around the globe. That is political power! It is a power that too many lamenting distractors, commentators, and scholars fail to see. Our we-ness has always been the very definition of "the huddled masses yearning to breathe free," even when we felt snubbed as European immigrants jumped in front of us to the head of the line. We recognize that without our fight, there would be no line for anyone else to get into.

This is what you attempted to describe in Memphis that fateful night. In panoramic language, you told us that we were one of many tribes and that we as people lead all kinds of clans, nations, and communities into the promised land—a land where all would be free to live, love, and labor with dignity. What you preached that night you heard stereophonically playing in your mind through Duke Ellington and Mahalia Jackson's soulful prayer:

> Lord, dear Lord above, God almighty,
> God of love,
> Please look down and see my people through.[17]

8

THE WORLD HOUSE

He's got a-you and me sister in His hands
He's got a-you and me sister in His hands
He's got a-you and me sister in His hands
He's got the whole world in His hands
—SUNG BY MAHALIA JACKSON,
"HE'S GOT THE WHOLE WORLD IN HIS HANDS"[1]

Martin,

Your assassination was arguably an attempt to end democratic revolution in the United States. The world since your death continues to be filled with oppressive and manipulative regimes that find it easier to crush dissent in the name of law and order than to seek justice. The civil rights battles for democracy that you feared would turn into a nightmare were, however, not for nothing. That struggle was world historical, and it continues to inspire democratic activism all around the globe. At home and abroad, people continue to engage in freedom struggles. I remind myself of this frequently when I reread your Nobel Prize Peace Prize acceptance speech.

I accept the Nobel Prize for Peace at a moment when twenty-two million Negroes of the United States of America are engaged in a creative battle to end the long night of racial injustice. I accept this award on behalf of a civil rights movement which is moving with determination and a majestic scorn for risk and danger to establish a reign of freedom and a rule of justice.[2]

This movement was as globally significant as Toussaint Louverture's epic battle against Napoléon's armies in the Haitian Revolution, where the people from below fought organized battles to end enslavement and the severest forms of human exploitation. Haiti's revolution was an earthquake. It shook Amsterdam, Antwerp, Buenos Aires, Copenhagen, Kingston, Lisbon, London, Liverpool, Madrid, New Orleans, and Rio de Janeiro. It put the fear of God—and of the people—in global powers. The Haitian Revolution, like the "Negro revolution,"[3] is too frequently minimized, its radicalness papered over, because these histories are a reminder that no power can govern only to its own advantage forever. All people have a right to the tree of life, and when circumstances change, resistance will arise from the ground up. Unlike Louverture, you saw the majesty in democracy. The "Negro revolution," as you called it, shook the "world house." You defined the world house as our global interconnectedness resulting from technology and communications. Global freedom struggles were as much part of what you termed our new global linkages. This is what you believed made the civil rights movement so vital a part of world struggle:

Along with the scientific and technological revolution, we have also witnessed a worldwide freedom revolution over the last few decades. The present upsurge of the Negro people of the United States grows out of a deep and passionate determination to make freedom and equality a reality "here" and "now." In one sense the civil rights movement in the United States is a special American phenomenon which must be understood in the light of American history and dealt with in terms of the American situation. But on another and more important level, what is happening in the United States today is a significant part of a world development.[4]

Democratic struggle has been an arduous one. It is an ancient one. The specific struggle that you and I were born into in the twentieth century commenced in the latter of half of the eighteenth century and went through the nineteenth century. The road to a democratic Oz, figuratively speaking, has been full of fits and starts. Monarchal rule throughout Europe consistently rejected liberalization. And this was true wherever centralized power was held. This spread of democratic ideals aligned with the rise of the nation-state, landed and linguistic boundaries formed into political entities—in the case of the United States, "a more perfect union." The US has always been an ethnically diverse and gender diverse union—containing West Africans, various Europeans, and Indigenous nations—but was governed homogeneously by an elite set of White, property-owning males whose families had made good on the spoils of conquest and slavery. It would take nearly fifty years of struggle to remove property ownership as a requirement for voting in the US. This left only a minuscule number of African American men—and no women—who could vote. Theoretically, citizenship in the United States is not determined by blood lineage. It is determined by allegiance. The Constitution is a bound oath, a secular assent to swear and uphold its tenets. Access to our national fellowship, however, was limited by labor, property, race, religion, and sexuality. So from the late eighteenth century through the twentieth century, an ongoing struggle raged to expand the limited boundaries of who could be a member of the republic, and under what terms.

This was a great transformation. Political obligation based on fealty to a monarchal system began eroding. Monarchs once globally ruled, heading multiple nations that were culturally, legally, and linguistically diverse. The idea of a singular nationality determining the fate of a state without a monarch challenged prevailing ideas of government. Today, we think of nationality and state as being synonymous—the French, the Ghanaians, the Indians. At that time, though, leadership and fealty were far more local and provincial the world over. The wealth generated by minerals and mass agricultural staples, such as sugar and silver from the Americas, deflated the riches of empires as far away as China. It is not as though monarchs did not jealously protect their monopolies; they did. But they were challenged by the burgeoning investor class that Karl Marx called the bourgeoisie. Marx's theorization was not fully accurate, but he was on to something as he viewed these patterns in the rearview mirror. Former British subjects in the colonies, such as the framers of the Constitution, desired to keep the empire's ill-gotten gains for themselves. Of course, there is more to the story, but the economic motivations too often are taken as a negligible aspect of this history in popular renderings. Democracy and capitalism slowly crept up and expanded around the globe. Proclaiming the need for democracy became one of the chief vehicles in shaping the modern nation-state. National citizenship did not need to depend on religion, language, or place of birth; it could be conferred as a matter of legality in the constitutional nation-state.

As Marx analyzed this system of economics and governance, he observed new forms of labor alienation and inequality. His front porch in Germany, and later England, had a narrow sight line. Though Marx could clearly see labor alienation and inequality, which became orthodox in Marxist thought, he was less attuned to the part race played in the shaping of bourgeois economics. The bourgeoisie engendered stronger divides along the lines of gender and race than class.[5] Instead of barbarians, as the ancients termed nonparticipants in governance, the new order that began with the conquest of the Americas made Blackness the marker of political nonparticipation. Blackness connoted enslavement, and across the globe, Black people were impugned as niggers. In the Americas, Black labor became the bellwether of early capitalism. These contours formed with the transatlantic slave trade, the centuries-long expulsion of Indigenous nations in North and South America, the corporate militarized takeover of India, and Europe's maniacal scramble to claim the African continent at the end of the nineteenth century—what the French cleverly termed the *fin de siècle*. Labor practices and racial isolation in cotton and sugar plantations throughout the Americas, especially in the American South, were replicated in the laboring practices the world over. Laborers "exchanged their country marks," their facial markings that once identified their clan loyalties, to borrow historian Michael Gomez's book title, for a newer, encompassing nationalism.[6] One India! Africa for the Africans! Pan-Arabism! Zionism! Colonization, economic exploitation, enslavement, and racism all midwifed more nationalist resentments.

At the end of the nineteenth century, W. E. B. Du Bois witnessed the formation of a global color line that had bypassed Karl Marx's analysis of capital. New technology enhanced the economic exploitation of people of color to fell, harvest, mine, and plant. To manage and maintain wealth, elites devised and revised schemas of racial taxonomy to explain their greed. Race, not as

nation but as biology, became essential. Though Marx was a witness to capitalistic disruption, he was oblivious to Eurocentrism.
It eluded him that capitalism was glued together by a cultural
chauvinism, cemented by a taxonomy of race and gender. This
was the petri dish that spawned the commercial order we live
in now. The physical laborers in agriculture, domestic service,
and mineral extraction from around the globe were and remain
the Atlases upholding the new capitalist world. Their realities
have been hidden and taken for granted. It was not until 1903,
at the height of a surging influx of European immigrants into
the United States, that Du Bois eloquently observed the truth
of this division:

> Herein lie buried many things which if read with patience
> may show the strange meaning of being black here in the
> dawning of the Twentieth Century. This meaning is not
> without interest to you, Gentle Reader; for the problem of
> the Twentieth Century is the problem of the color-line.[7]

Du Bois's insight was relegated to a US problem of "race relations" even though he keenly recognized it was a global concern.[8]

Europe's Enlightenment, its eighteenth-century ideas of scientific rationality, were driven by imperialist conquest. These ideas
were filled with gendered racism and were prejudicial from their
inception. This rationality was offered as fact, not hypothesis. All
the while, the capitalist reordering of the world was furthered
through governmental liberalization, privateering, and practical
technologies developed for resource and human exploitation. Karl
Marx was correct that "the discovery of America, the rounding
of the Cape, opened up fresh ground for the rising bourgeoisie."[9]
Yet Du Bois offered greater insight into how European worldly
philosophy jaggedly stitched the global color line, stating, "The

problem of the twentieth century is the problem of the color line—the relation of the darker to the lighter races of men in Asia and Africa, in America and the islands of the sea."[10]

In 1912 the openly racist Woodrow Wilson was elected president of the United States. Wilson's southern racism had been imprinted through his conservative Presbyterian rearing. So the defeat of the Confederacy was his apocalypse. As a child he witnessed a captured and bound Jefferson Davis, the former president of the Confederacy, being transported through Augusta, Georgia, to Fort Monroe. As a result, Wilson became the quintessential New Southerner, marketing the South's military defeat as the nobility of Southern heroism. Southern dominance of the US military was key to this propaganda campaign.

Through the military, the United States began exporting a global version of American apartheid that had been perfected in its conquest of the western US during and after the Civil War. Wilson's views were shaped between the Scylla and Charybdis of humiliating Southern defeat and westward conquest, which eventually led to an unconscionable, and all but forgotten, invasion of Haiti in 1915. It is laughable to think that Wilson might have awoken in the middle of the night, fearful of Haitian resistance to slavery led by Toussaint Louverture or Jean-Jacque Dessalines, with a machete at his throat. Anyway, demonstrations of US power used the lessons learned from anti-Black, -Brown, -Native, and -Asian racism to make apartheid globally palatable. How ironic that in 1917, when Wilson uttered to Americans that they were "making the world safe for democracy" by entering World War I,[11] he really meant that he was securing White American nationalism. He was aligned with, though some say he was hoodwinked by, European nationalist politics in a common interest to keep racial capitalism intact.

In 1917 the journalist John Reed fittingly titled his account of the Russian Revolution *The Ten Days That Shook the World.* The

Marxist paradigm, though limited in its governmental formulation, had what Cornel West insightfully described as "an ethical dimension."[12] West believed that Marxism had its pitfalls and had failed Soviet politics but, as a social theorization, had a moral compass contained within it. Gross inequalities ruled the world when the Machiavellian politician V. I. Lenin and his crew of roughnecks, the Bolsheviks, overthrew the czar's rule. The Bolshevik melee was naively cheered on around the globe by those who had seen their lives and lands crushed by the insatiable machinery of racial capitalism. Reed was right that this revolution shook the world just as the Haitian Revolution had done almost 125 years earlier. Now here was a political economy based on cooperation and that challenged the supremacy of unbridled capitalism.

In 1919 World War I came to an end, and the "great powers" negotiated a treaty in Versailles, France. These negotiations were not the apotheosis of democracy but rather its racist antithesis. They were not only a punishment for Germany's hubris but also a hostile takeover of German-held African colonies of Togo, Cameroon, Namibia, Tanzania, Rwanda, and Burundi.

Joseph Conrad's 1899 novella *Heart of Darkness* is set in the Congo, a colony privately owned by the king of Belgium. The story's chief antagonist, Kurtz, is mortified by his and European civilization's devolution. The equatorial sweat wrung from the daily brutality of colonialism is too much to bear. In the density of tropical forestation, Kurtz recognizes that nothing lasts. He is degenerating just like Europe's power. As he faces his own personal demise, he utters "The horror! The horror!" Kurtz's civilization was rotting.

Kurtz prophesizes. He is the ghostly figure giving witness to a racialized global order that European powers will quickly, in retrospect, lose control of. The hyena feed that took place between 1884 and 1885 at the Berlin Conference divided African people and lands without awareness of nations, hatreds, and languages. The seeds of collapse were sown, and Kurtz's lamentation foretells the nine million who will die in Europe during the First World War. That meeting in Berlin marked the beginning of the end for Western dominance.

White wrath seethed globally at the turn of the twentieth century. By the 1919 Treaty of Versailles, a combination of war weariness, wounded national pride, and unabashed greed took hold. Kurtz's horror was in full form. Across the pond, the United States had arisen as a global power. Its ascent as the leader of the West was in plain view. President Wilson enforced a variety of apartheid laws domestically and would encourage them in Versailles. Wilson's war to vouchsafe democracy was followed by urban pogroms from Chicago to Tulsa, a marine invasion of Haiti, and an Osama-Bin-Laden-like hunt for the revolutionary nationalist Poncho Villa through Mexico.

While the "darker races" were being corralled by forms of White imperialism, there was a breakthrough in the United States with the ratification of the nineteenth amendment, which removed gender as a barrier to vote. So, many women finally received the right to vote under this amendment. Like the motto of Frederick Douglass's newspaper, *The North Star,* stated, "Right is of no sex—Truth is of no color—God is the Father of us all, and we are brethren." This was necessary and long overdue, but in Georgia, where you were born, this did not apply to your mother, Alberta Williams, or a number of her cohorts. The women of her generation were still fighting racism alongside sexism, and this continues way past her death. The enfranchisement of women in the US predictably unfolded along the color line.

In frustration, Black folk have dreamed of their own separate racial democracy. Perhaps they had no choice. Roughly sixteen thousand people fled the United States for Liberia in the nineteenth century, many through the encouragement of the American Colonization Society, a group that mainly targeted free people rather than the enslaved. Many of these people hoped to build Black-led democracies. By the early twentieth century, some imagined transnational linkages with Ethiopia, India, and Japan. The struggles and successes of these countries somehow resembled Afro-America's, though very little was understood about the internal disputes and smoldering hatreds within each country. On the surface, they appeared as colored nations unconquered by Europe. Living with apartheid, Black folk could only dream of what it meant to be fully self-governing. Emperor Meiji, Emperor Menelik II, and Mohandas Gandhi were non-White leaders, nationalists fighting to maintain or gain independence and build their own countries, though it was conveniently ignored that they subjugated others in the process. It did not matter that they were militarist or xenophobic, given the madness of Eurocentrism. It is only in retrospect that this romance has been recognized as political oppression in other guises.

The wonderfully vainglorious Jamaican Marcus Garvey, along with his second wife, Amy Jacques Garvey, and the countless women who organized and trumpeted a global Black nationalist vision, marched to the slogan "Africa for the Africans" and offered a counternarrative to Black political impotence. In 1920 the Garvey-convened Universal Negro Improvement Association (UNIA) issued the *Declaration of the Rights of the Negro Peoples of the World*. In it they declared democratic freedoms on their own nationalistic terms. It was reminiscent of what Jean-Jacques Dessalines had done in 1804 in Haiti or Olympe de Gouges had done for French women in 1791. The UNIA leadership recognized that Black folk had to look within themselves for beauty, power, and political self-determination. Garveyites understood how Anglo-European dominance had been built using their labor and with material resources from their lands. Collective power was the only way to end subjugation. However misguided Garvey's nationalism was accused of being, it caught the attention of working-class Africans, Black Americans, and a variety of West Indians. Garvey's vociferous charm frightened both the Black bourgeoisie and the United States government—so much so that they colluded to destroy Garveyism. Marcus Garvey was deported. On December 2, 1927, ten thousand people waved goodbye to him from the docks of New Orleans. You were not yet conceived, but this was the world that awaited you and so many others who were born as the Great Depression fell upon a generation like a mushroom cloud.

Wall Street crashed in1929, just as you began to toddle. In the South, economic instability was even worse for those whose fate was tied to local cotton and its Jim Crow superstructure. And for urban dwellers, the economic pummeling often meant destitution. So many people were left homeless. Churches, like the one your father pastored, helped their people as much as possible, but the poverty was overwhelming. Your parents and kin tried to reduce your exposure to the most heinous parts of the Depression, but they could not protect you enough. In your hometown of Atlanta, you heard the names and stories of the Scottsboro Boys and Angelo Herndon. And racial brutalities continued throughout your formative years.

Your childhood was filled by bits of inspiration, arising from organizing, resistance, and even interracial cooperation. A. Philip Randolph and Milton Webster were the principal leaders of the Brotherhood of Sleeping Car Porters and Maids. In Harlem and Washington, DC, there were boycotts of local stores—"Don't Buy Where You Can't Work." Interracial unions organized in the Congress of Industrial Organizations (CIO) and the United Auto Workers (UAW), and legal victories were won by the NAACP.

Nevertheless, the politics throughout the South degraded Black people. From every southern state legislator, *nigger* was used with the same frequency as in gangsta rap records, but without the internal love and respect. And you, I am sure, have never forgotten performing, dressed as a pickaninny, with the Ebenezer choir at the 1939 premiere of *Gone with the Wind*. The church you would make world famous needed the proceeds.

As you approached your teens, the outbreak of another maddening world war appeared imminent. Democratic institutions in Germany, Italy, and Spain were collapsing from power-hungry lies. Truthfully, full democracies never existed in the majority of the world, including Europe. In 1919, as peace was being negotiated in Versailles, European powers insisted that there would never be a seat at the table for the colonized countries they ruled. Too many riches, too many spoils, too much servitude to be given up. Why ease the White Man's Burden with an emerging leadership class peripheral to the well-established interests and rule that were entangled through European capitals? While in Washington, DC, Woodrow Wilson's one great idea, the League of Nations, was being drowned in a US Senate bathroom by his isolationist archrival Henry Cabot Lodge.

What was left after the First World War were crumbling democratic institutions, too weak to challenge the rise of authoritarianism. Francisco Franco bombed his liberal opposition to death in Spain's brutal civil war, and Hitler rose to power with the desire to accomplish what Napoléon Bonaparte had failed to do. Germany's Weimar government had lost its traditionalist base. The German populace's long-held prejudices against Jews, the Roma, and homosexuality found renewed fervor in Hitler's ritualized hate. Genocidal megalomania filled the void where democratic institutions seemingly failed. In Italy dreams of Italy being recognized alongside its "elite" European peers drove Mussolini to try to conquer Ethiopia. He would form a bond with Germany's tyrant in a narcissist alliance. Pope Pious XII, who feared communism more than social injustice, connived with Germany, Italy, and Spain.

The erosion of civil protections and democratic due process, in a violent effort to make authoritarian governance acceptable, had a side effect. It allowed tens of millions to be crucified and devoured across the land masses of the earth. And in Japan, Emperor Hirohito's militarism rolled like lava across the Pacific countries, seeking dominance over Korea, China, the Philippines, and all the countries around the South China Sea. Hirohito's desire to control Japan's neighboring countries was the final straw leading to the Second World War.

The Second World War was Pandora's Box: once begun, it unleashed the greatest weapons of mass destruction. By the war's end, the world was split into factions. Winston Churchill gave his Iron Curtain speech during the year you entered seminary. Churchill declared that the spread of Stalinism would be disastrous for the Western world but said nothing about the rest of the world. His attitude was in direct opposition to the views you were forming. You wrote, "Christianity also insists on the value of persons. All human personality is supremely worthful. This is something of what [Albert] Schweitzer has called 'reverence for life.'"[13] Churchill desired to keep atomic weaponry out of the hands of his Soviet adversary, with no reverence of the lives of African and Asian people fighting to alleviate the Anglo-European domination of their nations. His concern was only how these nations related to the Soviet Union. He was blind to the color curtain that Richard Wright described. Like Conrad's Kurtz, Churchill saw the peoples of Asia and Africa as merely pawns on a page. Had he noticed that Fulton, Missouri, where he gave his famous speech, was racially segregated? His Cold War analysis was clouded with White.

British and American companies desired cheap produce, natural resources, and maximum profits, pumped from Iranian oil fields and plucked from bananas on Central American plantations. Though slavery had been abolished, these overlords continued to perpetuate and hide the workings of their pecuniary interests using Cold War propaganda. By the mid-1950s there were multiple secret wars waged against duly elected leaders by devilish government agencies, theoretically in the name of democracy. Ironically, democratic elected officials were being undermined left and right by protectors of democracy: Prime Minister Mohammad Mosaddegh of Iran in 1953, Jacobo Árbenz of Guatemala in 1954, and Prime Minister Patrice Lumumba of the Democratic Republic of Congo in 1961. Any resistance to this racial feudal order of the West was labeled communist. Churchill's Tory philosophy went down like a smooth southern bourbon at Fulton's Westminster College; it preserved the geopolitical color curtain.

Southern statehouses believed themselves to be wrapped in Jesus's shroud. They upheld God and country. These politicians, and the corporate leaders they legislated on behalf of, claimed that Americans were God fearing. In the southern political economy, the Black working poor were doubly taxed. The bifurcated social order preserved enough divisions that the wealthy could manage political dominance over everyone. It appeared as the natural order of things. In 1957, while civil rights protests and legal cases pressed for rapid legislative change and the year the Gold Coast renamed itself Ghana, the US paper currency was first embossed with "In God We Trust."[14] One can only guess that the formidable corporate and political idealogues believed the fear of God would halt citizens from taking up concerns about employment, endemic racism, and voting. Throughout the 1950s in the United States, being God fearing tended toward sloganeering rather than the realities of the law. Long-held anti-Asian, -Black, and -Mexican laws protected White wealth in God's name.

These men in gray flannel suits selfishly controlled committees of the Senate, the House, and their own big businesses. They were the real-life *Mad Men*. When the Afrikaner Nationalist Party rose to power in 1948 in South Africa, they were bolstered by the racist US Cold Warriors. Cold Warriors—whose admirals were isolationists, John Birchers, and Klansmen—believed that underneath every rock was a communist. Communists were like mosquitoes and had to be eradicated with the insecticide DDT—a poison that killed not only mosquitoes but other life too. God-fearing racial pieties were shibboleths that justified Jim Crow practices. Apartheid was birthed from this same God-fearing God-talk, just as it was in the United States.

This aligned with big-city politics in the US industrial belt. As WWII dawned, groups that were once considered the lower rung—Czechs, Italians, Irish, and Jews—became politically elevated through Democratic coalition politics. In the aftermath of the war, Catholics and Jews were gradually starting to enjoy a fully "White" status. Their entrance into the White fraternity meant they were no longer seen as suspicious radicals. They moved from controlling police and fire departments to leading precincts and wards to being mayors of cities and jealously guarding hard-won political gains, wrested away from the nativist establishment. Since Whiteness was the source of these groups' newfound cultural cachet, Black people threatened this power. And wherever possible, White ethnic political leaders attempted to subvert Black economic and political gains. In these cities, White ethnic politics helped to foster, through federal and local laws, Bantustans just as cruel as any in South Africa. It was cold war at home and abroad.

The term *Cold War* applied to Afro-America as much as to the former Soviet Union. The phrase was coined by Bernard Baruch, a multimillionaire South Carolinian turned New Yorker who advised presidents from Woodrow Wilson to Harry S. Truman. In

1947 Baruch used the term in a speech before the South Carolina Dixiecrat legislature to describe the frosted relationship between the Soviet Union and the United States over nuclear armament. But it also applied to Black citizens protesting legal apartheid. "Let us not be deceived," Baruch said. "We are today in the midst of a Cold War. Our enemies are to be found abroad and at home. Let us never forget this: Our unrest is the heart of their success."[15]

During your years of postsecondary education, folks of color everywhere were in an uproar. In 1947 Indians finally made the British relent their colonial rule. By 1949 Mao Zedong had won victory in China's civil war against his nationalist opponents. In 1952 Lieutenant Colonel Gamal Abdel Nasser led the Free Officers Movement to victory in Egypt, ending Britain's governing power in Egypt and Sudan. And the list of resisting countries goes on.

May of 1954 was auspicious. In Indochina Ho Chi Minh led the Democratic Republic of Vietnam's resistance army against their colonial ruler and exploiter, France. Ho Chi Minh, a nationalist politician committed to communism, believed the people of Vietnam could govern themselves without European interference. It was their right to organize and choose their structure of government. No one believed that the ragtag coalition army could defeat superpowered France, but it happened on May 7 at the Battle of Dien Bien Phu. There, arrogant French militarism was defeated, forcing France to withdraw from Vietnam. However, US Secretary of State John Foster Dulles and President Dwight D. Eisenhower did not yield on their neo-colonialist foreign policy efforts. Soon after the French packed their bags in Vietnam, Dulles and Eisenhower devised a different set of machinations that laid the ground for the United States' ten-year civil war in Vietnam, a war that distracted the country away from its own internal bigotries and impoverishment.

On May 14, seven days after Dien Bien Phu, you were called to be the twentieth pastor of the Dexter Avenue Baptist Church in Montgomery. You thought you were coming to a more sedate place to complete your dissertation and get a foothold as a Baptist preacher. Three days later, the US Supreme Court ruled in *Brown v. Board of Education of Topeka* that legalized apartheid in the United States was impermissible in schools. It formally ended ninety years of legal racial segregation. *Brown* gave impetus to the movement that sucked you into the vortex of world history. And years later, you would become one of the most recognizable dissenters of the US war in Vietnam.

By 1957 you had found hope in the collective efforts of Black Montgomery's resistance to bus segregation. You saw the possibility that Black people globally could be self-governing. This was confirmed for you when you attended Ghana's first Independence Day on March 6 as a part of the American delegation. You were inspired as you watched the black star flag rise and the British flag descend.[16] You hoped that Kwame Nkrumah's Convention People's Party could ally with other parties to bring the Gold Coast's diverse cast of nations together into a unified democratic state. Upon your return to the United States in May, you delivered a powerful message before thirty thousand people at the Prayer Pilgrimage for Freedom in front of Abraham Lincoln's monument, charging legislators to ensure that Black Americans had secure rights to vote.

The Second World War, though horrific, created space for Black Americans to exchange ideas alongside African and Asian colonials who were leading their respective independence movements against Anglo-European colonization. Black lives were connected to all other laboring lives around the globe. Afro-America's rich internal diversity, the variety of complexions, hues, and shades, was indeed an expression of global connectedness.

You pragmatically recognized that democracy has been an integral part of Black life in the United States. Black folks' blues were blues felt in some form or fashion all over the world. In the world house, Black American struggle was never isolated; it represented the possibility that working people could overcome and make their world safer for democracy. In your 1964 Nobel Peace Prize acceptance speech, you recognized your unnamed ground crew, who sacrificed to make democracy a living reality.

The next year, 1965, the poet Langston Hughes, analyzing two hundred years of Black American poetic history, observed that the "color problem is a drag on the whole world," not just the United States.[17] The Anglo-European coalition, led by the United States through a complex web of military alliances, national economies, and greedy interests, reluctantly supported the ill-advised US strategy. The Vietnam War was much costlier than the Korean War, its precedent. Cold War madness descended around the globe from Angola, Congo, Cuba, Egypt, Ghana, Guatemala, and Iran to the barrios, ghettoes, and hollows in the United States. Political cynicism grew as the United States intervened in the governance of other people. The coups, the espionage, and the wars they supported undermined the promises of democracy.

On that spring evening when you were murdered on the Lorraine Motel's balcony, your murderers believed their troubles had been subdued. They wishfully thought that by eliminating you, they would end centuries of democratic abolitionism. Their actuary calculations were correct to a limited extent. It is easy to kill the dreamer, but the dream cannot be killed unless you kill every single dreamer—and even then, the dream is an idea that echoes around the world.

Governments are too often maintained by myths, that mix of fact and fiction that allows us to take for granted the world around us without much examination. Every system is sustained by a collage of aspirations, beliefs, faiths, and rituals. This is why leaders fight so vigorously to defend their positions by basing them in some kind of faith—patriotic rituals, church hierarchy, the sanctity of the holy word. The powerful are in a never-ending struggle to maintain their legitimacy and cultural normalcy—that the way things are set up are the way they should be. The elites fear the loss of their dominant status, and so they rush to inflame public anxieties to panic levels to uphold their questionable schemes of privilege. Franklin Delano Roosevelt, an elite in his own right, noted in his most famous presidential address, "The Four Freedoms," that the fourth most important thing about freedom is to live without fear. "A good society is able to face schemes of world domination and foreign revolutions alike without fear," he exhorted. He projected geopolitical fear as it related to foreign adversaries. However, his words spoke to a greater truth: "Freedom means the supremacy of human rights everywhere."[18]

Without a full sharing of power, people lose faith in a governing system; it dies as ignobly as the czarist family, the Romanovs. And it is axiomatic that ruling authorities in every age refuse at some point to detach themselves from destructive elements in their origin myths. As you opined, quoting the nineteenth-century Scottish historian Thomas Carlyle, "no lie can live forever."[19] Though they can live for centuries! This was the great genius of Abraham Lincoln. He moved the country forward by repurposing its mythic origin through the Declaration of Independence. You observed, "Nothing could be more tragic than for men to live in these revolutionary times and fail to achieve the new attitudes and the new mental outlooks that the new situation demands."[20]

You, however, stepped with democratic faith into the world house, an international society interconnected through air travel, computing, and faster networks of communication. As a Baptist preacher with parochial congregations in the cities of Montgomery and Atlanta, you preached and acted upon what countless elite academics only ever pontificated about.[21] Your public charge was to expand, reorient, and reinvigorate our common faith in democracy itself so it could be actualized. You understood that freedom struggles have affinities across the globe.

> Along with the scientific and technological revolution, we have also witnessed a worldwide freedom revolution over the last few decades. The present upsurge of the Negro people of the United States grows out of a deep and passionate determination to make freedom and equality a reality "here" and "now." In one sense the civil rights movement in the United States is a special American phenomenon which must be understood in the light of American history and dealt with in terms of the American situation. But on another and more important level, what is happening in the United States today is a significant part of a world development.[22]

Today we face greater challenges to all humanity with the ecological dangers of climate change. The overheated atmosphere has jeopardized the entire planet. The inability to think morally about our habitation is an even greater challenge today than when you were alive. Climate change has been built upon all the sins of greed, militarism, and racism that you openly worried about during the last two years of your life. The world house itself is imperiled. This is why you asked us to practice a form of democracy grounded in selfless love. You recognized it took faith, a daily and devotional constancy, to redress social injustices and abusive legalities. You understood, like we must today, that it is a daily existential leap to build democracy in our world house:

This call for a worldwide fellowship that lifts neighborly concern beyond one's tribe, race, class and nation is in reality a call for an all-embracing and unconditional love for all men. This oft misunderstood and misinterpreted concept . . . has now become an absolute necessity for the survival of man. When I speak of love . . . I am speaking of that force which all of the great religions have seen as the supreme unifying principle of life. . . . As Arnold Toynbee says: "Love is the ultimate force that makes for the saving choice of life and good against the damning choice of death and evil. Therefore the first hope in our inventory must be the hope that love is going to have the last word."[23]

Love must guide our political conflicts, choices, philosophy, and strategies. This, you believed, would keep all of us alive and in the light.

9

ALL LABOR HAS DIGNITY

Hold it right there while I hit it
Well reckon that ought to get it
Been
Working and working
—SUNG BY NINA SIMONE,
"CHAIN GANG (WORK SONG)"[1]

Martin,

I can still hear your resonant voice speaking to the sanitation workers in Memphis:

> So often we overlook the work and the significance of those who are not in professional jobs, of those who are not in the so-called big jobs. But let me say to you tonight, that whenever you are engaged in work that serves humanity and is for the building of humanity, it has dignity, and it has worth. One day our society must come to see this. One day our society will come to respect the sanitation worker if it is to survive, for the person who picks up our garbage, in the final analysis, is as significant as the physician, for if he doesn't do his job, diseases are rampant. All labor has dignity.[2]

Although all labor is good, the labor of the working poor has never been dignified.[3] It has been abused, cheapened, and exploited. At the heart of slaveholding systems are abused laborers. Entire civilizations are built upon labor exploitation—American, Greek, Roman, and countless more. The truth is that labor has always been cheapened by greed, no matter the contemporary form it takes. The historical sociologist Orlando Patterson called this thief "natal alienation," at birth the things of your own hands are pried out of them by a master.[4]

During the Reformation, both Jean Calvin and Martin Luther tried to reclaim the idea of work with the theological notion that God gives each person a vocation. Each person has a God-given calling in the labor of their hands. Each person must use their talents creatively to enhance God's creation. This meant that each laborer had to be attentive to their work, and this was a wonderful theological sentiment. Calvin's argument upended the Roman Catholic paradigm in which one's labor status was permanently fixed. One need not thrive but could be satisfied with one's God-given station. According to Calvinists, one's labor was attached to God's benevolence, the end of which was human salvation. In Calvinist doctrine, labor is essential to Christian vocation. The effort derived from the works of our hands—creative, mental, and physical—are a grateful response to God's love and grace. How well one performed one's work was indicative of God's indwelling and redemption.

In the 1530s, as Calvin feverishly wrote his *Institutes of the Christian Religion*, Spain reached the border of the Inca Empire. The Spanish slowly replaced the Incas as the dominant political rulers of the region. Spain's rule was abusive, especially after the discovery of the great silver mines in Potosí, Bolivia. Many Indigenous laborers did not believe in a theology that saw labor as a calling from God. Their exploitation in the mines came from a cruel God. Those who adopted Catholicism—forced upon them by colonists—came to see the crucified Jesus that hung in the sanctuary walls in their local parishes as a comfort in enduring their physical toll. Their labor was not vocational; it was oppressive.

Spain's less powerful sibling, Portugal, nearly turned their sibling rivalry into outright warfare. In 1493 the Roman prelate brokered the Treaty of Tordesillas, which kept these siblings from descending into a fracas in the Americas. By 1549, however, the Portuguese monarchy found a greater spoil in its colonization of Brazil's Native nations. They would be the first European power to systematize sugar in the Americas. The introduction of sugar required laborers, and those laborers would be brought from the coasts of West and West Central Africa. The Portuguese monarchs' coffers overflowed.

One hundred years later, Calvinist theology traveled with the Dutch, English, and Scottish preachers, traders, and thieves into the Caribbean and North America, ramping up the religious enmities and economic competition with their Catholic rivals. Though Calvin espoused high regard for labor, avaricious historical realities tell another story. Dutch merchants, English dissenters, Huguenot refugees, and Scottish rum dealers were all a part of the Calvinist slave-trader elect. But what about all the nonelect who were kidnapped into the Americas? What of their birthrights? What of their alienated labor?

Calvin's influential theology infused human productivity with an ennobling quality. Work was sanctioned by divinity; it was no longer sheer drudgery. Vocations like agriculture, carpentry, and shoemaking offered a larger purposefulness. They were a blessing, a sign of the divine's loving intent. Interestingly enough, this is an idea Karl Marx and Friedrich Engels absorbed from Calvin. Like Calvin, Marx and Engels thought there was something sacred regarding human labor and how it was directed. For them, desacralized labor was alienated labor, and capitalism was the sin that upended the meaningfulness of labor. While Calvin's positive assessment of labor was affirming, ironically, the countries that welcomed Calvinism—Britain, Germany, Holland, Scotland, and the United States—turned out to be the most exploitative and alienating toward human labor as the Industrial Revolution commenced. Calvin's high view of human labor did not convince the lords of his era, as it has not convinced the lords of our own.

However, as Black preachers and prophets of liberty made Protestantism their own, they too preached the dignity of labor. They recognized that too few Black laborers were dignified. They, like you, commented on the cruel laboring conditions. In 1831 Maria Stewart thundered from Boston's Franklin Hall:

> Few white persons of either sex, who are calculated for anything else, are willing to spend their lives and bury their talents in performing mean, servile labor. And such is the horrible idea that I entertain respecting a life of servitude, that if I conceived of there being no possibility of my rising above the condition of a servant, I would gladly hail death as a welcome messenger. O, horrible idea, indeed! To possess noble souls aspiring after high and honorable acquirements, yet confined by the chains of ignorance and poverty to lives of continual drudgery and toil. Neither do I know of any who have enriched themselves by spending their lives as house-domestics, washing windows, shaking carpets, brushing boots, or tending upon gentlemen's tables. I can but die for expressing my sentiments; and I am as willing to die by the sword as the pestilence; for I am a true born American; your blood flows in my veins, and your spirit fires my breast.[5]

The Presbyterian clergyman Henry Highland Garnet picked up on Stewart's views. He saw slave labor as a violation of the Christian sabbath. To willfully inflict ceaseless work upon people and steal their birthright did not accord respect to God or God's people. This gross violation of labor was plain and simple thievery. Powerfully, Garnet called for mass revolt and resistance to this blasphemous human degradation:

> SLAVERY! How much misery is comprehended in that single word? What mind is there that does not shrink from its direful effects? Unless the image of God be obliterated from the soul, all men cherish the love of Liberty. . . . The divine commandments you are in duty bound to reverence and obey. If you do not obey them, you will surely meet with the displeasure of the Almighty. He requires you to love him supremely, and your neighbor as yourself—to keep the Sabbath day holy—to search the Scriptures—and bring up your children with respect for his laws, and to worship no other God but him. But slavery sets all these at naught, and hurls defiance in the face of Jehovah.[6]

By the twentieth century, Black laborers earned grotesquely low wages throughout the South. In addition, the convict leasing system put men and women in jail on trumped-up charges, only to have local governments cheaply lease them out as laborers to individuals and private corporations to pay off their sentencing. This in fact reenslaved many Black people to brickyards, chain gangs, coal mines, cotton fields, and pine forests—without political participation.[7] In 1939, as the US quietly ramped up to enter World War II, Mary McCleod Bethune, one of the greatest unsung leaders in US history, opined that racist labor exploitation was undemocratic:

The democratic doors of equal opportunity have not been opened wide to Negroes. In the Deep South, Negro youth is offered only one-fifteenth of the educational opportunity of the average American child. The great masses of Negro workers are depressed and unprotected in the lowest levels of agriculture and domestic service, while the black workers in industry are barred from certain unions and generally assigned to the more laborious and poorly paid work. Their housing and living conditions are sordid and unhealthy. They live too often in terror of the lynch mob; are deprived too often of the Constitutional right of suffrage; and are humiliated too often by the denial of civil liberties. We do not believe that justice and common decency will allow these conditions to continue.[8]

Black struggle has been perennially about the dignity of labor.[9] Black labor in general, whether in enslavement or domestic services—child rearing, construction, cooking, cleaning, elder care, and farming—has been cloaked by invisibility. And Black women's essential labor, beginning with the loving Mammy figure, has been socially disregarded even until this era of "essential workers." Women's labor has always been triply taxing, with responsibilities in child rearing, domestic and field work, and income generation. In 1937 Zora Neale Hurston famously summed up in *Their Eyes Were Watching God* that Black women are the "mules of the world." She had seen Black women in her anthropological fieldwork in Haiti and throughout the US South as well as in her life in New York City do backbreaking toil with the least, or no, compensation. There was no Fair Labor Standards Act for these women. But for all of their labor, Black women were the most disrespected of the working class. Two years before Hurston's *Their Eyes*, Ella Baker and Marvel Cooke published their 1935 investigative report, "Bronx Slave Market," in the *Crisis* magazine:

Rain or shine, cold or hot, you will find them there—
Negro women, old and young—sometimes bedraggled,
sometimes neatly dressed—but with the invariable paper
bundle, waiting expectantly for Bronx housewives to buy
their strength and energy for an hour, two hours, or even
for a day at the munificent rate of fifteen, twenty, twenty-
five, or, if luck be with them, thirty cents an hour. If not
the wives themselves, maybe their husbands, their sons, or
their brothers, under the subterfuge of work, offer worldly-
wise girls higher bids for their time.[10]

With hardheaded analysis, Claudia Jones in 1949 wrote "An
End to the Neglect of the Problems of the Negro Woman!" to
challenge the Communist Party and a large readership to take
seriously the lives of Black women as workers. She observed:

In 1940, two out of every five Negro women, in contrast to
two of out every eight white women, worked for a living.
By virtue of their majority status among the Negro people,
Negro women not only constitute the largest percentage of
women heads of families, but are the main breadwinners
of the Negro family. The large proportion of Negro women
in the labor market is primarily a result of the low-scale
earnings of Negro men. This disproportion also has its
roots in the treatment and position of Negro women over
the centuries.[11]

Like Hurston, Claudia Jones surmised that "Negro women—
as workers, as Negroes, and as women—are the most oppressed
stratum of the whole population."[12]

Novelist Ann Petry, with unsparingly gritty realism, captures
the brutal angst of living as a single working woman and mother

in Depression-era Harlem in *The Street*. Petry's protagonist, Lutie Johnson, observes:

> And while you were out working to pay the rent on this stinking, rotten place, why, the street outside played nursemaid to your kid. The street did more than that. It became both mother and father and trained your kid for you, and it was an evil father and a vicious mother, and, of course, you helped the street along by talking to him about money.[13]

It is true that all labor has dignity, but in practice, it is a lie. It is a lie because women workers are neglected globally. This sexist racism is in the contemporary political branding of "crack hos," "skeezers," and "welfare queens."[14] These derogatory terms are buttressed by the ever-present typologies of female slave labor in the plantation South.[15] Every Black woman is someone's affable loud-talking Mammy or an insatiable Jezebel. The reality was that both the stereotypical Mammy and Jezebel worked from sunup to sundown and were the backbone of the planter political economy. The lives of Black women as laborers, especially nonprofessional ones, were dismissed calculatingly in policy and mocked by public imagination and corporate promotion.

Though you always recognized the difficulties of laboring men and women, you too often discussed the problem only in terms of male wage earners. Black male dignity is so evocatively captured in those Memphis photographs, which can now be found all around the Internet, of protesting sanitation strikers armed with a sign stating I AM A MAN![16] The powerful truth behind that signage was only half the truth; Black women bore painfully low wages too. And their labor was given no expression in that protest at all. There were no protest placards stating I AM A WOMAN!

Recognizing the shifting future of industrial labor, you warned the United Auto Workers in 1961:

> New economic patterning through automation is dissolving the jobs of workers in some of the nation's basic industries. This is to me a catastrophe. We are neither technologically advanced nor socially enlightened if we witness this disaster for tens of thousands without finding a solution. And by a solution, I mean a real and genuine alternative, providing the same living standards which were swept away by a force called progress, but which for some is destruction.[17]

You initiated a Poor People's Campaign without full consideration of the greater concern of women in your community. It was not until the women of the National Welfare Rights Organization (NWRO) confronted you about the depth of sexism in social welfare policies in both the New Deal and the Great Society that you began to wake up to the linkages between low-wage labor and assistance programs. Johnnie Tillmon, one lead organizer of the NWRO, educated you on the need for guaranteed income and family assistance.[18] Tillmon was not buying the moralistic appeals to the male-centric Protestant work ethic. She understood, through lived experience, that women did a great deal of essential work—such as child-rearing and care for the elderly—without wages.

Tillmon, like you, also came to understand—even before machines displaced Black laborers off the plantations with the introduction of the cotton picker—that automation was deeply affecting the efforts of Black women to support their families. In 1948 the mechanical cotton picker was employed to deal with the Second World War labor shortage.[19] The draft and labor migration from the South to the North destabilized the cotton industry. This date commenced the long death of low-wage physical labor as a necessity in the US economy. The mechanical cotton picker foreshadowed what would happen to laborers throughout the United States. Industrial labor unions did not pay much attention to the plight of Black and Brown laborers in the South, Southwest, and West until the plague was upon their own houses. Thirty-two years later, factory laborers would join displaced farm workers in the service economy. Soon the Midwest, a region where Black southerners migrated in order to make more money, would be on life support.

There were 159 domestic rebellions throughout the United States in 1967. The post–World War II economic boom had reached its ebb. The surplus laborers coming from the South were intentionally excluded from the industrial economy. By then, US manufacturing had begun to feel competition from Germany and Japan. These factors, combined with endemic racism, continually frustrated Black communities and kept them on lockdown. From the 1969 election of Richard Nixon to the election of Ronald Reagan in 1980, the acute national and global competition that the United States faced was unwisely ignored by politicians and corporate leaders. These critical issues, which dated back to policy choices of the 1930s, plagued urbanized Black folk in their attempts to consolidate political power in cities and towns across the country.

The NWRO was a democratic vanguard. They demanded guaranteed income for laborers being displaced by automation and childcare support for working families with children. They insisted that federal family assistance programs be truly supportive of families, no matter their configuration—single parents, unmarried parents, or same-sex cohabitants included. Their radicalism grew out of poor Black women's economic invisibility.

Their economic importance went unchartered, ungraphed, and undocumented. The dismal science, as economics is called, was focused on the captains of industry, who were always White men, and male industrial workers. Economics as a discipline took women's labor for granted. Yet it was so-called women's work—childbearing, childcare, elder care, farm work, household labor, and the transaction of sex itself—that pumped untold wealth into the economy. It was these undignified women, as women on welfare were considered, who radicalized your understanding of political economy.

The faults of unbridled capitalism were not a "father knows best" scenario of male wage earners or business owners. From 1954 to 1960, the hit television sitcom *Father Knows Best* reflected the ideals of a political economy led by middle- and upper-middle-class White men. This show was a funny fantasy. The fault lines in an unbridled economy would eventually undermine the uneasy status of White male wage earners like the father in the show. The women of the NWRO, the lowest on our social ladder, helped you see this and embrace their struggles and understand how legislation pushed by Great Society and New Deal politicians punished them for being women, mothers, and childcare providers.

Leaders of the NWRO inversed the Gospel of John's vignette of the woman at the well. Jesus tells of the polyandrous woman who visits the well in the middle of the day instead of early in the morning, as was the custom of women. She fears the gossip and the scorn that her partnerships provoke in her community. In the patriarchal society, she does not dare show her face. Her sexual arrangement is considered shameful, and she is scorned, much like poor Black women have been in the US. In a sense, the women of the NWRO were the daughters of the well, and they made you understand their social and economic ostracization even within their own communities. Your exchange with these leaders led you to grow more radical and to more fully appreciate how poverty is enmeshed in a narrative of racism and sexism. By 1967, your views were shifting. You began to envision the intersections of gender labor, race, religion, and technology in a capitalist taxonomy constructed on Black women's backs.

Liberal social scientist Daniel Patrick Moynihan bastardized Black mothers further. His infamous report to President Lyndon Johnson purported to explain the problems with "matriarchal headed families."[20] Moynihan, even by the standards of his time, seemed completely unaware of his intellectual biases against women, especially Black women. He compared, in all his East Coast arrogance, his own fatherless life as an impoverished Irish American to Black histories. The latter are in stark contrast to Irish immigrants, who had been shaped by British political subordination, the gendered hierarchy of Roman Catholicism, and an ability to assimilate into Anglo-American Whiteness. Whereas Black folk were the national outliers. Regardless of disparate backgrounds and family cultures, Moynihan determined that the father-knows-best White patriarch would be best for Black families to emulate. Moynihan, and others of his ilk, flattened our collective histories. Neither Moynihan nor lawmakers did Black families any favors. Instead, they punished Black people, Black women especially, for not conforming to norms that never existed in their own kinship networks.

The forceful presence of NWRO leaders challenged your ignorance about the gendered realities of women's labor. You knew nothing of what it meant to live under patronizing state and local rules for buying baby formula. Powerful men built their reputations passing condemnatory legislation against poor Black women in the United States. Even case workers, who were overwhelmingly women, aligned themselves with the patriarchal rules that governed poor women's lives. State disapproval of poor Black women extended to an insidious critique of the Black men who loved and fathered their children. They were not "real men," according to the punishing state legalities. Real men, meaning White men, could fiscally take care of their women without state largesse. This bourgeois logic, vehemently coded in anti-Blackness and reinforced by one-sided statistical data, was rehearsed, recited, and rehashed—*Papa was a rolling stone, wherever he laid his hat was his home.* Black laziness was reinforced so much that Black people believed it and disapproved of their own low-income and despairing relatives.

You knew from living in a Chicago West Side tenement the depressive conditions of impoverishment. You and Coretta quickly came to understand what Ann Petry's character Lutie felt like being trapped in a dank life of immobility. Reflecting on your summer of living in the Lawndale community of Chicago, you observed about your children:

> Our own children lived with us in Lawndale, and it was only a few days before we became aware of the change in their behavior. Their tempers flared, and they sometimes reverted to almost infantile behavior. During the summer, I realized that the crowded flat in which we lived was about to produce an emotional explosion in my own family. It was just too hot, too crowded, too devoid of creative forms of recreation. There was just not space enough in the neighborhood to run off the energy of childhood without running into busy, traffic-laden streets. And I understood anew the conditions which make of the ghetto an emotional pressure cooker.[21]

You saw how those conditions affected your children and you quickly returned to Atlanta. This sense of alienation that you described taking hold of your children was the greater alienation that comes from being trapped in a matrix of sexist, racist, and prejudicial narratives. This alienation destroyed the sacred in each of us. Black women struggling in neighborhoods like Lawndale understand how these damning narratives are central to the alienating conditions they faced. In the last months of your life, you were connecting dots. It slowly began to dawn on you that Black American women were lightning rods as to why economic inequities maintained undemocratic political order. Black women's laboring histories represented a far wider global truth about the lives of the poor everywhere.

The weeks before you were assassinated, women, men, and children gathered at Mason Temple to hear you give support to sanitation workers who were on strike. You affirmed their protest by saying that all labor has dignity. However, you also knew that behind those working poor men were working poor women—aunties, domestic partners, friends, lovers, mothers, sisters, and wives. They were more invisible than the narrator in Ellison's *Invisible Man*. They were forgotten. Your labor support was noble, but it did not go far enough.

Today these women, along with fellow male laborers, are called essential workers. People value them because they worked servicing many during a dreadful pandemic. Their work kept grocery stores open, mail coming, and buildings and streets sanitized. Folks all around put up yard signs thanking them for their service. Yet too few people have fought to increase these essential workers' wages and benefits to keep them and their families fully healthy.

The ever-growing problem of cheapened labor, as our ancestral enslavement foretold, is that it cheapens people and the institutions that abuse them. This is why we must remain vigilant and think through the actual patterns of labor that distort the democratic impulse.

So we must face a bitter truth. Most labor is not dignified. The democratic struggle before us is to dignify all labor, acknowledging Black women by making their work visible and recognized. The US economy is continually scheduled by inequitable algorithms. The most exploited labor is invisible to the wider public. We in the United States are the beneficiaries of mines in Eastern Congo; factories in Bangladesh, China, and Vietnam; and extractions from poor communities at home. Our democratic aim, as it was yours, must be to make the rules governing labor more transparent. A just democracy must be intentional about exposing labor inequities and protecting collective bargaining as a right of all working people. This is key to sustaining a spirit of democracy.

I love the sentiment that "all labor has dignity." It inspires me still. It is a hope, but not yet a reality. Our daily spiritual warfare is to make all labor dignified. Organizing the essential workers of our communities continues an ongoing struggle. You had prescience when you wrote:

> In days to come, organized labor will increase its importance in the destinies of Negroes. Automation is imperceptibly but inexorably producing dislocations, skimming off unskilled labor from the industrial force. The displaced are flowing into proliferating service occupations. These enterprises are traditionally unorganized and provide low wage scales with longer hours. The Negroes pressed into these services need union protection, and the union movement needs their membership to maintain its relative strength in the whole society. On this new frontier Negroes may well become the pioneers that they were in the early organizing days of the thirties.[22]

10

GROWING UP KING

Time is truly wastin'
There's no guarantee
Smile's in the makin'
You gotta fight the powers that be
—ISLEY BROTHERS, "FIGHT THE POWER"[1]

Martin,

"Growing up King," as your son Dexter wrote, was never easy.[2] My generation shared the trauma of living as the children of the civil rights generation. Night after night in living color, even above your pleas for nonviolence, we witnessed the volcanic overflow of a violently changing society. There was the Vietnam war and its protests and the civil rebellions in Chicago, Detroit, Newark, Watts, and countless other cities. These sparks of change engendered political violence against and in reaction to our struggles for the simplest of democratic freedoms. People of my generation can chant the activists and martyrs in an incantation—Louis Allen, James Earl Chaney, Mark Clark, Addie Mae Collins, Medgar Evers, Andrew Goodman, Fred Hampton, Bobby Hutton, Jimmy Lee Jackson, the

Reverend George Lee, Herbert Lee, Viola Liuzzo, Carol Denise McNair, James Reeb, Carole Robertson, Michael Schwerner, El-Hajj Malik El-Shabazz, Emmett Till, and Cynthia Wesley. We, however, could never feel Yolanda's, Martin III's, Dexter's, or Bernice's immediate terror when you, their uncle, and their grandmother all died horribly. As Jamil Al-Amin, formerly known as H. Rap Brown, said, "violence is as American as cherry pie."

Violence is too familiar. It bends our posture, makes us warily look over our shoulders, attentive to gunshots, and fearfully not allow our children to play outside. We know the sources—the auction blocks, addictions, deprivations, domestic abuses, imperial defeats, poverty, and ever-present misandry, misogyny, and racism. These are forms of PTSD, living among us and within us. These are our realities. This was true throughout your lifetime, and it will be true long after your death.

The lessons of nonviolence that you advocated were lessons we need to internalize in our daily affairs. I am reminded of Charles Burnett's 1990 film *To Sleep with Anger*. The film centers on long-lost family member Harry, played by Danny Glover, who is welcomed after surprising his relatives in Los Angeles with an unexpected visit from down South. Harry appears genial, but his visit is ominous. His intent is to wreak havoc on the family's domestic tranquility and usurp his cousin's lives. Once Harry is invited in, he refuses to leave and fuels misapprehensions between parents and children, husbands and wives. Burnett ingeniously uses folklore in the film to explore the ways that Black families who left the South cannot escape the traumas they left behind. These traumas have a way of popping up unexpectedly, as personified by Glover's character.

The characters are burdened with deep fears, confusions, and hurts endured from a brutally coercive past.[3] New and old wounds from "down home" all factor into how families cope with the everyday harshness of 1990s South Central Los Angeles. As you know, Martin, our all-too-human wounds were the things we carried as we migrated North, South, East, and West. Burnett's film reminds us that adverse spells hover over Black communities even as we sleep. Harry, the shadowy family visitor, is a reminder that we have always had our external and internal struggles. Racism in a capitalist society plays havoc with our sense of self and value. And this sense of worth provokes in us angers that we often fail to examine. Harry's foil is Suzie, played by Mary Alice. She is the one who is politically committed, willing to self-sacrifice to end the devious trickster and internalized hatreds that lead to the destruction of family and community. Her Christlike bloodshed saves the family. She offers no grandiose speech about the greater Black struggle. Her power comes from an inner light. Of course, Burnett's film falls into the trope of a Black superwoman making oblations on behalf of her community. Whatever the shortcomings of the film, it's her quiet self-sacrificial act that heals the trauma.

The word *trauma* finds its origin in the word *defeat*. After your death, we were traumatized. It felt like we were defeated, and the only emotion we had left was rage—at yet another murder of an activist and spokesperson without justice. It left an unhealable, gaping wound. Like the characters in *To Sleep with Anger*, we as a community tried to bury the past of racist injuries only to see them triggered by the next case of police brutality, the next Klan rally, the next political dog whistle, the next small act of personal aggression in school or on the job. Racism, from the personal moments to the structural systems, keeps us traumatized. This ever-shifting set of ideas that draws negative distinctions within humanity according to ancestry and phenotype limits personal opportunity and democratic freedoms. This cruel infliction of humiliating and harmful ideas has been internalized. Black folk, too, blame one another for the feces of history that landed on us. Though we are constantly resisting racist stigma, it has been exhausting trying to prove our worthiness. So we have slept with our angers. You furiously asserted at the Lincoln Memorial:

> One hundred years later, the life of the Negro is still sadly crippled by the manacles of segregation and the chains of discrimination. One hundred years later, the Negro lives on a lonely island of poverty in the midst of a vast ocean of material prosperity. One hundred years later, the Negro is still languished in the corners of American society and finds himself an exile in his own land. And so we've come here today to dramatize a shameful condition.[4]

But anger is double edged. Outwardly it manifests in our restive struggles for an inclusive democratic society. Internally, however, anger festers into self-blame and self-recrimination. It depresses us because we evaluate ourselves by a false materialism, or to use your phraseology, we "thingify" ourselves through measurements that never satiate our longing for life, liberty, and the pursuit of happiness.

Too many of my generation did not appear attuned to the realities of our times. The racialized economy that our parents, your generation, pinned their hopes on was quickly withdrawn with the shuttering of auto plants, steel mills, and stockyards. We hoped that we were "gainin' on ya" as P-Funk sang in "Chocolate City," but the reality was devastating divestiture that shattered our middle-class dreams.[5] As your namesake, Martin Luther, is said to have claimed, "What the right hand giveth, the left hand taketh away!"[6]

The timing of our births after World War II has always meant we were dual citizens. On the one hand, by no doing of our own, we belonged to a democratic republic that granted us limited access to citizenship. On the other hand, we were viewed as a threat in a zero-sum game of racial politics. It was the *White* working class, not the solidarity of the working class as a whole. This kind of logic continued to pit interests of different ethnicities against each other. As we struggled to persevere and be included, we were demarcated as a national antithesis. To add insult to injury, our political trials and triumphs were intentionally diminished in the telling of US histories. This is why books like Lerone Bennett Jr.'s *Before the Mayflower* gave life to so many of my generation. These people's histories affirmed that we existed.[7]

Our struggles, it seems, could have been pulled from Thomas Hobbes's *Leviathan*, a seventeenth-century political musing amid the English civil wars. The constancy of living in a Hobbesian warlike state is exhausting. Truthfully, most of us desperately want quiet normalcy. We want to forget our never-ending democratic defiance. We crave to "all get along." In recent years historians have produced a bevy of scholarship on late 1960s and early 1970s Black radicalism. However, the greater truth is most Black folk did not appreciate and were not themselves radicals. Most folk wanted to exist unnoticed in the dominant society. We wanted to pass.

Passing is a derisive term among Black folk. It connotes those who could run away from the poverty and racism linked to Blackness. They are family members who avoid the darkest members of the family. But notions regarding passing have always been more complex. There is an entire literary corpus discussing what it means to pass in the United States. Passing stories are tales of those who tried to avoid the Atlas-like burden of holding up an unwanted racial inheritance. In James Weldon Johnson's 1912 *Autobiography of an Ex-Colored Man*, the protagonist discovers his enslaved heritage as mixed-race child and tries to understand to what group he belongs. The main character in Danzy Senna's 1998 *Caucasia* seeks acceptance by her Black friends despite her light skin. And Hollywood had its own versions of the tragic mulatto. In Douglas Sirk's 1959 remake of *Imitation of Life*, a white-skinned daughter runs away to escape the stain of Blackness, and Elia Kazan's 1949 *Pinky* is the story of a nursing student who crosses the color line and returns South to visit her Black laundress grandmother. These stories of passing tell us more about how race is lived in our society.

And then there are my generation's passing stories. O. J. Simpson declared, "I'm not Black; I'm O.J."[8] Simpson believed his extraordinary athletic abilities gave him a pass from the quagmire of living with racism and that he could bypass being politically committed to building a better democracy. In the end, they did not. Like the characters in the films and novels in the previous paragraph, Simpson had to face his own deeply disturbing demons as well as come to terms with the racial boundaries of American society. These passing stories are an acknowledgment of the emotional torment we constantly face. We simply want to use whatever means necessary to escape the incessant torture of having to think about our place in the national obsesssion with pigmentocracy.

Even though many of us have wanted to pass, we were pulled into a battle we had not made a conscious commitment to fighting. We were told by elders, grandparents, and parents that it was our responsibility to keep up the fight. However, most of us had not taken enough inventory of ourselves and our circumstances to figure what battles we were fighting. The truth is, many of us simply want to blend—be accepted by and be like those in power. Thus we have often felt more captured by the struggle than liberated by it.

Our King years were entangled with struggles of national independence and local self-determination. The election of Black city-council members, the expansion of congressional representation, the election of mayors, and the efforts to control local education, fire and police departments, and economic capital were all fought to advance dimensions of democratic freedoms. These struggles did not abate after your death, they intensified. By the 1970s, the lives of Black children seemed cheaper and more expendable to legislatures. The 1968 Kerner Commission, which was appointed by President Lyndon Johnson, reported the severity and inequality in the US. Sadly, Johnson refused to accept the commission's report, in what I have come to believe was childish recalcitrance because it proved your critique of his administration in your "Beyond Vietnam" speech to be correct. The inequalities expressed in the Kerner report only worsened.[9]

From 1968 through 1975, there was plenty of discussion of Black liberation, but somehow it did not make its way to the general public.[10] It did not inform our philosophical or spiritual understanding of social good. Truth be told, too many of my generation were sucked into a materialist vortex promoted by a diverse set of characters: from the University of Chicago economist Milton Friedman to New York City's great prayer warrior of capitalism Rev. Ike. These prophets of materialism as freedom joined with a political conservatism in order to bury idealism based in collective interests. And it worked. Safeguards and safety nets were ripped up like the trolley tracks that General Motors snatched up! By the 1980s, a new Malthusian theology of cruelty had an open road.

Since the eighteenth century, ruling elites in both England and the United States have used Malthusianism to justify unconscionable levels of economic inequality. In 1798 the Reverend Thomas Malthus, an English cleric, asserted that poverty was due solely to the poor's improvidence—in other words, the poor's bad behavior justified their own impoverishment. Malthus's moral postulation regarding population and poverty is rarely challenged and pops up everywhere. Malthus, who lived off the imperial beneficences of Great Britain, never thought to ponder other variables in his formulation of human population growth. He was yet another rich

English clergyman justifying a theology of cruelty.[11] Underneath our country's inaction on poverty is a theology, an understanding that God loves the rich and hates the poor, especially the Black poor.

In *Locking Up Our Own: Crime and Punishment in Black America*, James Forman Jr. describes how some Black people have supported the war on crime, which unjustly targets poor Black men, and investigates the causes of this. In an interview with NPR, Forman gives a poignant vignette of a Black judge who admonishes a young offender and subsequently sentences him harshly:

> And then he wrapped up, and he said, so I know you've had it hard, but people fought, marched and died for your freedom. Dr. King died for your freedom. And he didn't die for you to be running and gunning and thugging and carrying on and embarrassing your community and embarrassing your family. No, son, that was not his dream at all. So I hope Mr. Forman is right. I hope you turn it around. But right now actions have consequences, and your consequence is Oak Hill. And he locked him up.[12]

This judge held a code of honor over the young offender. Now, the judge had every right to feel outrage at the young man's offenses. However, the judge used you as a punishing yardstick. Did he understand the structural violence and divestment that surrounded the young man's behavior? Invoking your name was done to punish, not enlighten. The judge enshrined notions of individual character without seeking an alternative restitution to the crime the young man committed. It is as if the judge had read about you through Shelby Steele's 1991 book *The Content of Our Character: A New Vision of Race in America*.[13] The judge, like Steele, suffered from a shallow understanding of the structural and individual realities within the United States.

We who grew up King shared the joy and the burden of keeping the dream alive, though we never defined what the dream meant politically. Unfortunately, the dream became characterized by consumerist desires. We were no different than other Americans in this regard. We substituted consumerism for political commitment. This has been an ongoing problem. At the height of the 1963 Birmingham desegregation campaign, organizers had to threaten consumers with public shame to keep them out of stores for Easter. This boycott strapped retailers and forced them to come to the table to negotiate the end of segregation. Large retailers got the last laugh, though, as the protest made them more money in the long run. Sometimes I feel that we are more interested in the right to shop than in what political liberation means in a democratic society. This problem has only grown.

We must accept that we are and have been in constant warfare for place and station in our society. This double consciousness, as Du Bois called our societal bipolarity, this incongruency, distracted a generation. It kept many of us from seeing the ultimate purpose is democratic self-governance with ultimate respect and care for one another. Stuff on steroids—automobiles, clothing, gym shoes, and jewelry—displaced politics and philosophy. It is not that material status is unimportant, but materialism has never fed the soul. Our concern for building institutions that fed inner humanity was taken for granted, something you warned us about:

> And there is always the danger that we will find ourselves caught up in this foolishness. We must always be careful in America because we live in a capitalistic economy, which stresses the profit motive and free enterprise. And there is always the danger that we will be more concerned about making a living than making a life. There is always the danger that we will judge the success of our professions

by the size of the wheel base on our automobiles and the index of our salaries rather than the quality of our service to humanity. There must always be a line of distinction between the "within" and the "without" of life.[14]

Chasing materialism without spiritual moorings to guide our pursuits prevented us from soberly envisioning the institutions we needed to build and rebuild. And this, combined with the ambient White noise of racism, caused us and our children to spend forty years in an inward wilderness of self-blame.

Our refusal to accept a Pollyannaish narrative of a more perfect union has been costly and a constant challenge. In 1969 President Richard Nixon's speechwriters cleverly came up with the idea of a "silent majority" in seeking support for his continuation of the Vietnam War. Since prominent Black leaders like yourself opposed the war, the term applied doubly. Just who were the unpatriotic "outspoken minority"? Who had been leading the revolutionary charge throughout the South and in the urban core of US cities? Whose sons were dying disproportionately in the war? When Muhammad Ali stated, "I ain't got no quarrel with them Vietcong,"[15] he was correct. However, White conservatism tried to drown him out, just as conservative commentator Laura Ingraham tried to do with NBA all-star LeBron James when she told him to "shut up and dribble."[16]

A people born of democratic struggle can never be blindly devoted to the patriotic sloganeering ginned up by dissembling politicians and their stooges. We must always take a knee to nostalgia. Supreme power, like Nixon and his ilk desired, requires fealty, not governing consent. Nixon played on fear and used societal disjuncture as a political weapon to maintain power. Conflicting histories are resolved by the "silent majority." On the other hand, the first Black president, Barack Obama, had the opposite problem. He tried to create a shmaltzy consensus history. Conflict, however, is democratic too. Where truth is at issue, there can never be an absolute consensus.

In the internal histories of Black folk, allowing for voice, having a voice, and the uniqueness of voice is our gift to theories of democracy. The distinct mixing and mashing of voices continues to be one of our greatest influences: bebop, bluesy lamentations, disco, funk, gospel, hip-hop, jazz, jug bands, rag, soul, and spirituals. This has been our calling card. "I, too, sing America," the first line of Langston Hugues's poem, "I, Too," is an anthem. It challenges forms of political singularity or domination. Everybody has the right to join the chorus and sing, the right to tell their stories, speak their truths, and sing their way.

Our experiential parsing of the Protestant Bible, along with the creation of spaces to live among ourselves, helped us to creatively reimagine ourselves as a political community. Through our religious and fraternal orders, we fostered our own sacred histories. This is what brothers James and J. Rosamond Johnson captured in "Lift Every Voice and Sing."

> God of our silent tears,
> Thou who has brought us thus far on the way,
> Thou who has by thy might,
> led us into the light[17]

The realities of democratic struggles are enormous. And they will continue into the future as new technologies and techniques are devised to control the masses and enrich an elite few. The powerful will prolong methods that coerce, dictate, mute, and surveil to maintain political dominion. This type of political power is in direct opposition to a democratic philosophy of "lift every voice."

As I analyzed the events over the course of your life and in the wake your death, I realized that Black folk of my generation were naive. In the United States, Black Americans have always been the working poor, at best. In 1960 only 3.1 percent of Black Americans had completed college or postsecondary education. By the time of your death, that had edged up to 4 percent. And today it is hovers roughly around 15 percent.[18] This increase is wonderful. However, it means that most Black communities continue to be working class. In the late 1960s, after your death and when public activism for corporate jobs and boardrooms began to fade, many were, like Stephen Carter's eponymous book title, "affirmative action babies." We were fortunate enough to gain access to majority-White academic institutions. Black activism throughout the 1960s opened doors to those of us who had the fortitude to endure constant questions from professors and students alike implying that we did not belong in centers of learning predominated by White elites.[19] Throughout the 1970s, we fought retrenchment. In 1978 the US Supreme Court slowly began dismantling affirmative action in the *Regents of the University of California v. Bakke* decision. They were all telltale signs of the conscious attempt to politically erode access to an emerging Black middle class filled with dreams of self-fulfillment.[20]

There was some truth in calling those of us who lived through the 1970s the "me" generation, as coined by writer Tom Wolfe's in his celebratory homage to individuality in the excesses of the late 1960s and early '70s—drugs, rock, and the so-called free love that ended 1950s repression.[21] And there was real soul-searching in historian Christopher Lasch's morose critique of "the culture of narcissism" in his eponymous book as he reflected on US society in the wake of World War II and the unmooring of the self from connectivity and communal bonds in favor of a permanent adolescence. His intellectual search for a kind of selfless neo-Puritan commitment was much discussed at the time. However, neither writer had Black folk in mind, and they did not take seriously the kinds of questions that Black activists, artists, intellectuals, and writers were asking about community and democratic inclusivity. Nevertheless, in the immediate post-Vietnam era, neither did we in the emerging middle class. Too many of us believed we had arrived and that our success was due to our own efforts, even as we faced assorted institutional hostilities.

Narcissistically we were enticed by the conservatism of Malthus's cruel economics. We blamed Black people, rather than the rotten racial pathology of our society, for poverty. We succumbed to a prosperity gospel. We gleefully thought that a handful of first-generation college graduates could overcome systemic forces without the support of a base of political power. We lived in denial. We bought into Horatio Alger stories without ever having read one because it beat being the underdog. This is why we have clung to the rags-to-riches tale. And this is why we love our preachers—Creflo Dollar, Daddy Grace, Rev. Ike, T. D. Jakes, and the late Johnnie Colemon. They give us a weekly injection of prosperity. Success is easier to swallow than constant struggle. It is easier to try to hit the lottery than build a bank. Though Booker T. Washington has gotten an undeservedly bad reputation, we are in truth his heirs in the way we consider capital and democracy. Jay-Z projects a more secular, extreme version today, without the Protestant anchoring of Washington's considerations of wealth, in this lyrical utterance:

> Financial freedom my only hope
> Fuck livin' rich and dyin' broke[22]

Washington was right—and perhaps Jay-Z is too—that an individual's work ethic and business acumen are important. But the singular logic of accumulating capital and building wealth in and of itself has never provided guiding principles to build or live in a democratic society.

The truth is that we who grew up King were required to make space for multiple voices to sing in the choir. Freedom could never mean behaving anti-democratically like those who hold dominion. Our political commitment, which we too often forgot, is to lift all voices in our communities and encourage the same throughout our world. We know what it means not to be seen or heard. In other words, we must organize, reorganize, and rebuild community so that all can sing in our democratic choir.

Democratic freedoms have always meant more than living a middle-class lifestyle or behaving like we are the superrich. Of course, this is a truism, yet so many of us who grew up King forgot the strenuous demands that democratic struggle places on us. Instead, we focused on proving our social value through accumulation, as though we were not innately deserving of being dignified because we exist as persons. This attitude has taken a withering toll. And sadly, it is still reinforced by internalized self-loathing. This is why social commentator Michael Eric Dyson chided the Black middle class in a response to Bill Cosby's "Pound Cake" speech. In that speech Cosby excoriated poor Black youth for not living up to middle-class propriety, a feat he could not necessarily live up to himself.[23]

Middle-class moralization, incubated in a hothouse of religious ideals, was reduced to strict behavioral standards as the summa cum laude of faith. The emphasis on individual behavior conforming to the demands of the social order fostered a set of judgmental attitudes on moral and social dilemmas, rather than the considered insights of love as the evaluative standard by which to appraise the world around us. That kind of limited valuation has been quick to judge disease, poverty, and youthful hedonism as a matter of individual bad choices or morality. In other words, it kept so many in the emerging middle class from facing the realities that addictions, destabilizing economics, HIV/ AIDS, and other social traumas were not Black people's failure but the failure of institutions within our collective democracy. It was Malthusian theology at work in our political adversaries' favor. As a society, we were ashamed of ourselves for not being "the model minority," quiet, dutiful, and well behaved like some immigrant groups were falsely deemed.[24]

Successive generations of Black youth were expected to be more powerful than Atlas. If Zeus had commanded Atlas to uphold the race instead of the sky, he would have been crushed. Far too many souls have been blanched like dry bones in a desert in their efforts to prove their humanity. We are all already fully human; foibles and strengths are our birthrights too.

In 1963 the Birmingham Children's Crusade was deemed con- troversial for taking youngsters out of school to protest the city's segregation and allowing them to be jailed. This action defied *manly* notions of who was supposed to defend Black communities. What the vociferous critics of the Children's Crusade failed to acknowl- edge was that, without children, the Birmingham movement would not have successfully drawn attention to the Black South's version of apartheid. Activist youth, like Barbara Johns, the Little Rock Nine, and Bobby Hutton, have been combatants in democratic freedom struggles too. Children who are born into unjust condi- tions are rarely afforded the luxury of sitting out political struggle. Among Black children, especially the poor, policing begins early in every way imaginable. Either one learns to negotiate degrees of assimilation—code-switching and passive aggression—or one dies rebelliously on city streets without a cause, acting on pent-up frustrations or the exciting glamour that comes from living outside the boundaries of what the elders deemed respectable and virtuous.

Virtue is always dicey. We may have integrity in one aspect of our character but not in another. It is a daily struggle to be morally consistent. Living in a messy world requires more than individual character. The best any of us individually can do is to be self-aware. Roxanne Gay's book *Bad Feminist*, a collection of essays that examines the contradictions of a strict feminist ideology, is a worthy read for all of us. Our personal nobility is always prismed through assorted lusts, egotistical aspirations, insecurities, manias, and traumas. Our individual virtue may be well intended, but in the end, it offers little protection to those persons and people who have different experiences than we do. Civility, as professors Danielle Allen and Stephen Carter suggest, is the rule that allow us to discuss our differences without warfare. Courtesy and formal language that acknowledges our respect for one another is a way of securing our democratic institutions and protecting our chords of freedom.[25] We must strongly consider our political commitments as not solely to political parties but to freedom itself. Freedom, you stated, was the goal:

> I close by saying there is nothing greater in all the world than freedom. It's worth going to jail for. It's worth losing a job for. It's worth dying for. My friends, go out this evening determined to achieve this freedom which God wants for all of His children. No matter how much money you're making, stand up for freedom. I tell you this afternoon, I would rather be a . . . free pauper than a rich slave. I would rather die in abject poverty with my convictions than live in inordinate wealth a mental slave.[26]

Of course, we are not to be blamed totally for our political misunderstandings. They came directly from the pages of *Ebony* magazine. This magazine showed us forms of middle-class excellence within our reach. Those pages were revolutionary for many of us. They allowed us to see celebrity and fine brick mansions. They documented our own internal struggles about physical beauty. But what the pages of *Ebony* unwittingly reinforced was that the struggle was solely about individual accolades, not political community. At *Ebony*'s zenith in the 1960s, the magazine penetrated nearly every Black household. Ironically it was in the pages of *Ebony* that you were puffed up as "the Lawd," as some civil rights activists called you with mocking derision. Lerone Bennett Jr., the magazine's editor and fellow Morehouse College alum, wrote a hagiography of you with the mythic title *What Manner of Man*. The magazine regularly publicized you as the main face of the movement, if not the movement itself.

This was subsequently reinforced by your wife, Coretta Scott King. She nobly fought for Black people until her own death. Without her leadership, the remaining protests in Memphis would have been in shambles as men in the background jousted to step into your leadership void. She is never given enough credit. Here I must take a moment to personally make my own admission of sexism: I often felt then that she played the grieving widow too often. My false assumption blinded me from seeing her as a political leader in her own right. Dean Lawrence Carter of the Martin Luther King Jr. International Chapel at Morehouse College said that she was one of the greatest lobbyists in US history.[27] She tirelessly worked the halls of Congress and statehouses. This is why you married her. You assessed that she "was always stronger than [you were] through the struggle."[28] She was a woman of her own strong opinions and remained committed to the cause long after your death.

She led the King Center for Nonviolent Social Change and wanted it to have a bigger role as an institution for your vision of nonviolent activism. However, without millions and millions of dollars in endowments, it was very difficult to secure a political institute for social change. The King Center would soon shift its emphasis and focus its fundraising campaigns to enshrining your legacy. Though her politics were as substantive as yours, enshrining your legacy became her central organizing effort. She aimed to make your birthday a national holiday.

When your eponymous holiday was signed into law by President Ronald Reagan, Coretta stood over him with a victorious smile. She had handed the Reagan administration a stinging public defeat. It was a joyous moment of triumph over a conservative president who began his 1980 campaign running on the doctrine of "states' rights" that harked back to the old Confederacy. Though the victory was sweet, there was an irony in it. You were turned in that process into a legend. Legends are static; flesh and blood is not. You were an icon, and the problem with icons is they can foster cynicism. No one can live up to a historical image. Though discomfited, I understood why rapper Lupe Fiasco irreverently wrote and tweeted out his lyric "Fuck Martin Luther King."[29] His impertinence was no different than any working-class man who heard "I Have a Dream" and responded, "Fuck the dream, Martin. Tell us about the jobs!" You, as the legendary leader of the civil rights movement, wound up becoming a punishing yardstick, a moralization about how young people were supposed to behave. The political actions of your generation became myth. The veneration of you became more important than what you actually believed, did, and said. Icons over time are buried under candle smoke. Your true saintliness was obscured.

What is often overlooked is that the civil rights movement was about the reconfiguration of democracy. What the countless known and unknown leaders like you did was to make a commitment to democratic political struggle, the struggle to give voice and voices to a people. That was their altar call! Not only did they put themselves in harm's way, but they also put their families in the line of fire. What was most salient about you as a political actor was your self-aware political commitments. You died working daily to end the intersection of poverty and racism. You dashed from one place to another trying to keep a democratic movement positively invigorated. Your political commitment, no matter how flawed we may find it today, was to liberate the people you loved.

Too many of us who grew up in your immediate shadow believed that we could bypass making full political commitments. We confused commitment with simply voting, as important as that is. We, too, became cynical about democracy. It seemed better to recite the self-help motivation "think and grow rich." However, benign neglect, the idea offered by Daniel Patrick Moynihan to ignore Black protesters, took its toll.[30] The political activists among us constructively turned our eyes to the Free South Africa Movement. However, instead of continuously working alongside African people to build democratic institutions across our respective continental divide, protesting in front of the South African embassy and being arrested became a cause célèbre. It was performance. Our shared victimization at the hands of colonization and unfreedoms is what linked us. Empty moralizing about Black folk and Africa became a convenient substitute for engagement.

Those of us who grew up King came into a world brimming with democratic possibilities and a hope that two-thirds of the world's people might achieve governance of their own choosing. The civil rights generation was a minority within a minority who took on the conscious burden of challenging the ruling order. Without their commitment, Black communities would have remained resentful, subjugated, and unfree. We owe those named and unnamed a debt of gratitude. Gratitude, however, is not demonstrated by creating holidays, naming buildings, and erecting monuments. Gratitude is shown in the tedious scaffolding of institutions that foster free spaces for generations to come to lift up their concerns.

None of us were ever asked our consent to shoulder the responsibility of the past. Life does not seek our permission. Just like you, we were not asked whether we wanted to engage in democratic struggles. In an idyllic world, we would be able to choose our own paths. History, however, is not idealist philosophy. In a flawed constitutional democracy, we citizens are expected to make a difference. There may be powerful forces blocking the change we seek, but we the people are a force to initiate change. It is in our democratic engagement that life is worthwhile.

We would do well to remember James Russell Lowell's hymn "Once to Every Man and Nation," one of your favorites:

> Once to every man and nation
> Comes the moment to decide,
> In the strife of truth and falsehood,
> For the good or evil side.[31]

Life is and always will be challenging. Powerful ruling minorities perpetually attempt to control how the rest of humanity should live and what resources they should share. Generation after generation, we must face up to this collective challenge.

The lesson learned is that each of us is responsible for facing and recalibrating our political realities. This is a start of a political commitment. The other lesson is to accept the bitter truths of historical pasts. History's grand civilizations are filled with brutalities. To face these requires an inner fortitude built on the daily practice of loving our neighbor as ourselves. This is weight lifting that builds a type of muscularity. Strength, toughness of mind, and a healthy skepticism are our exercises. Black suffering unites us and connects us with those who live undignified. This is the wisdom of our shared histories.

Sadly, too many of us continue to be seduced by money instead of the agency that democracy provides. No doubt, economics are important. We need material assets to live, but a good life requires more. This is where you were at your finest, when you showed us that political commitment comes through tireless service. You summarized this commitment well in eulogizing your own life:

> I'd like somebody to mention that day that Martin Luther King Jr. tried to give his life serving others.
>
> I'd like for somebody to say that day that Martin Luther King Jr. tried to love somebody.
>
> I want you to say that day that I tried to be right on the war question.
>
> I want you to be able to say that day that I did try to feed the hungry.
>
> And I want you to be able to say that day that I did try in my life to clothe those who were naked.
>
> I want you to say on that day that I did try in my life to visit those who were in prison.
>
> I want you to say that I tried to love and serve humanity.[32]

This is how democracy stays alive.

11

THE CONTENT OF OUR CHARACTER

Hush, now, don't explain
You're my joy, and you're my pain
My life is yours, love
Don't explain.
—Billie Holiday, "Don't Explain"[1]

Martin,

Publicly you were virtuous, but privately you were incongruous—as we all are. You were part of the generation of Black middle-class men who hid behind respectability to cover over a multitude of sins—childhood humiliations, emotional confusions, lusts, and spousal abuse.[2] While plenty of things have changed for women in US society since the country's eighteenth-century founding, our national sexual politics highlights multilayered fault lines.[3] We must never forget that the privacy of our own homes offers lessons in democracy too.

Sigmund Freud, the mid-nineteenth-century Viennese pioneer of psychoanalysis, excavated patriarchal images that governed relationships between men and women. Freud's sexism, as we know today, made his theories flawed. Nevertheless, he understood that ideas buried beneath our consciousness factor into our outlooks and behaviors. He perceptively explored the sexual politics, frustrations, and tensions that lay below the surface of bourgeois culture. If Freud had had a chance to study the United States, he would have observed a country troubled by myths of racism and sexism, affecting both private and public decorum. Herein is the paradox for bourgeois males: even when we are behaving with apparent public equanimity, our personal relationships may be misguided by unexamined patriarchal myths.

In *Malcolm and Martin and America*, the theologian James Cone attempted to account for your and Malcolm X's maleness in the chapter "Just Men."[4] Cone explains that your behavior toward women typified men of your era. Both you and Malcom X viewed women's role as being supportive of males both publicly and privately. Though you were deeply influenced by liberal criticism that challenged biblical literalism, you leaned on one typology in the book Genesis, where Eve is described as Adam's helpmate. In this religious regard, Cone let you both you off the hook. What were your theological views about women? What did they say about the God you and Malcolm respectfully served as ministers? And what did that God have to say to women about justice and being full democratic citizens? Like Cone, I can only speculate that you would have grown had you lived longer. I am almost certain that your respective daughters would have invigorated that growth too. Cone's rather cursory interpretation of your masculine behavior as being "just men" is inadequate.

Men are never "men" by themselves. Maleness is defined in relation to femaleness. It is difficult to have full inclusion in a democratic society if myths about women in our communities and in our lives abound. To counter these myths, we must argue that our private intimacies, the personal mutualities between couples, families, and friends, and our public selves, must work congruently. Unexamined mythologies, as Freud surmised, fill our ideological sense of self as well as the body politic. The fearful biblical myth that Samson will be shorn by a deceitful Delilah affects how we think and live democratically. It fosters a political and cultural misogyny that women must be controlled politically as well as sexually. It is time we go beyond this, but Black men and women unfortunately continue to be chained to a sexual politics that does not reflect what democracy in theory must uphold—mutuality and love for one another.

In the 1970s feminist commentator Carol Hanisch argued in her essay "The Personal Is Political" that feminist politics was not simply a women's therapy session; it was the clarification of politics. In their 1974 statement, the Combahee River Collective brought more clarity to this phraseology: "There is also undeniably a personal genesis for Black Feminism, that is, the political realization that comes from the seemingly personal experiences of individual Black women's lives."[5] Our intimate struggles mirror the limits of our public imaginings. Being democratic requires an introspective examination of how we treat one another domestically, for democracy requires an ethic of mutuality. We must respect and provide room for one another. This is especially true when we do not fully understand what motivates ourselves or others. Our individuality is queerly opaque, and we are unknowable even to ourselves.[6]

Communal institutions, such as businesses, militaries, and religions, mold our beliefs and behaviors. Many of them challenge our personal autonomy. Institutions are designed to conform us, and not all conformity is bad. Rules of the road offer safety. Emergency drills provide protection. Schools teach us civic decorum. Religion shapes ethical behavior. However, there are limits. Institutional structures can also reinforce mandates that are less than loving. Holy writs, if we do not critically assess them, may be used in support of violent, repressive crusades. Violence silences, whether it comes in the form of harsh misogynistic sermon, ill-tempered corporal punishment, state-sanctioned death sentences, or dissent-stopping rubber bullets and tear gas cannisters.[7]

The content of our character is defined by how we reconcile our public and private selves. Thus we must strive to make them coherent. How do we live transparent and intimate lives at home and in the public arena of political decision making? How does intimacy mesh with publicness? What is the difference between a sensationalized tabloid exposé of personal struggles and public policy? A "society at peace with itself"[8] requires discernment between what is personal and what is public. The two can bleed into each other. There is always another side to all of us.[9] Our relationships are formed inside of communities—homes, neighborhoods, churches, clubs, and temples. Routine rituals inform our everyday attitudes. These are the ones we rarely explore, unless sniping at the personal life of a public figure. No matter how much we wish to separate these spheres, our personal intimacies are involved in the struggle for democracy.

The role of women in your intimate life is too often left to sensationalism. We forget that you were surrounded by women in intimate ways beyond your extramarital sexual dalliances. Their lives in relationship to yours help us understand democracy both publicly and privately.

The first woman you ever knew was your mother. Alberta Christine Williams King was born in 1904. Biographers offer very little in the way of your mother. She, unlike your father, never wrote a memoir.[10] What is remembered is that she was gunned down in Atlanta while playing the organ at Ebenezer Baptist Church. The culprit, Marcus Wayne Chenault, a mentally ill assailant, shot your mother on Sunday, June 30, 1974. Frenzied by voices in his head, he yelled, "You must stop this! I am tired of all this! I am taking over this morning!"[11] Your mother lived in the shadow of you and your father, though she was politically shrewd and calculating in the family business of Black Baptist politics, a business she was duly attending to when Chenault's inner rage left your family traumatized.

Your mother was born as racial segregation solidified. Howard University historian Rayford Logan called the moment "the nadir of American race relations."[12] Your mother was born into an extraordinary family. She was the daughter of an entrepreneurial Black Baptist preacher, the Reverend Adam Daniel Williams, and an ambitious mother, Jennie Celeste Williams. Together they built Ebenezer Baptist Church on Auburn Avenue. The Williams family could have been exhibit *A* in W. E. B. Du Bois's Parisian exhibition from 1900.[13] Only one of their children survived: your mother.

In September of 1906, just nine days after your mother's second birthday, the Atlanta riot was ushered in by journalists and politicians desperate to corral Black socioeconomic mobility. In a two-day pogrom, White Atlantans made Black Atlanta subservient. Luckily, the hot-tempered, defensively minded, less-than-respectable poor Black working people fought back and limited Black casualties.[14] It could have been worse. Here is a bit of irony: In today's Georgia, the right to bear arms is unreasonably defended. However, in your mother's second year of life, the state sent militia to disarm Black people and arrest over 250 Black men. Auburn Avenue was the street of Black ambitions. The riot was meant to kill those ambitions, but it failed. Your grandparents continued to grow Ebenezer alongside other prominent institutions of Black ambition.

You were close with your mother, Alberta Williams King. According to your sister Christine, you learned your invaluable listening skills from your mother.[15] She listened to you too! You discussed with her the women you dated and other intimate details of your daily life.[16] She set your expectations about what a spouse's role should be. She was a graduate of Hampton University (then called the Hampton Normal and Industrial Institute). By any measure, she was among Du Bois's leadership class, the Talented Tenth. Her Hampton education reinforced domesticity. An accomplished organist and pianist, she was educated to be a bourgeois Protestant woman. That education seemed ideal for a preacher's wife.

Behind the cover of family life, your mother was a fiercely political woman who understood the struggles of her city and the specific needs of the Black Baptist women. But in historical narratives, she is always an afterthought to your strong-willed father, Daddy King. Yet it was your mother who introduced you as a young clergyman to Black women's organizations within the National Baptist Convention; the great Black Baptist church leader Nannie Helen Burroughs was one of your mother's dearest friends.[17] This network ultimately helped you circumvent Black clergy members who were conservative, jealous, and recalcitrant about public protest—much like your father. So it was the church women, like your mother, who were the unsung stalwarts of the civil rights movement. Their political power helped transform the United States.

Like your father, you viewed your mother's role in bourgeois cultural terms, which shifted emphasis away from family as a wider network to one that was nuclear and solely headed by a father's income. Your mother likely reinforced those values. This is how her parents tried to live. After all, men were the head of the household in the Bible. This is how male dominance was sacralized, though women were crafty politicians inside and outside of the home, persuading, cajoling, and stealthily organizing to secure and maintain positions of institutional power. Your mother, like so many middle-class Black women of her era, was restless for self-autonomy and public respect for their leadership roles.

Women such as your beloved grandmother, Jennie Celeste Parks Williams, wrestled with these problematic assigned roles too. She was born just as Reconstruction was being suffocated by vigilantism. Your great-grandparents were born under the yoke of slavery. Your grandfather, Adam Daniel Williams, was born during the last days of enslavement and was fourteen years older than your grandmother. By the time they met, he had taken his ministerial ambitions from the rural Georgia countryside to Atlanta. They would form a church partnership and marriage, and eventually built Ebenezer Baptist Church together.

Your grandmother meant everything to you. Like you, she died carrying out service to her people. Tragically she died of a heart attack while giving the Women's Day sermon at Atlanta's Mount Olive Baptist Church. Her death made you so distraught that you attempted suicide. Somehow you believed it was your fault. However, if you had had time to look back on your relationship with your grandmother, you might have realized how much you were in fact like her. While she accepted the seeming normalcy of gender relations, your grandmother contested this sexism in her own way, joining the women's movement within the Women's Baptist Convention.[18] Those Women's Day church gatherings hid fraught power dynamics between male preachers and leading church women.

Your sister, Christine King Farris, had a challenging reality too.[19] It is forgotten that she had to deal with you as a younger brother, two years her junior, who graduated with her the same year, 1948. None of us will ever know the internal family dynamics, but it seems to me your sister might have felt overshadowed.

She was accomplished in her own right. Graduation could not have been the only time Christine had to share her limelight with you. Born to a dynastic legacy of preachers, you, the wunderkind, were preparing to be a conscientious leader of the family business. While you may not have been able to see all the undercurrents within your family system, I am sure she did from her vantage point as a Black woman.

These dynamics of family were infused in your marriage with Coretta, your beloved Cory. Like you, she was southern born and well educated. You were attracted to Cory because of her intellect, as well as her light beige-brown skin, even though the women in your family were deeper chocolate. In your mind, Cory was the ideal woman. You thought she would make the perfect preacher's wife.

The preacher's wife had to be a politically minded manager of a church as well as the day-to-day caretaker of household life. Black preachers' wives, however, were hardly ever submissive, vulnerable women. Although middle-class Black women did not have the suburban neurosis as described in Betty Friedan's *The Feminine Mystique*, they had their own worries about the gendered racism of American society. They worried for themselves and for their daughters. They faced acutely traumatic issues of abandonment, domestic brutalities, unemployment, unplanned pregnancies, and sexual assaults. These traumas were compounded by being both Black and female.[20] Black women's anxieties spread to communal concerns for their vulnerable brothers, cousins, fathers, husbands, lovers, sons, and uncles, who too often walked out the door to an early death. Preachers' wives wielded power and influence among other women within their local communities and congregations. From that position, they understood the limitations of their own men, especially the male preachers, and the dangers of the racist and sexist regimes that they faced.

However, Cory proved you were right: she was an ideal marriage partner. She was a strategic and independent thinker and a graduate of Antioch College, whose history of gender and racial equality began the day the institution opened its doors in 1853 under the presidency of Horace Mann. There she was exposed to contemporary leading activists and artists. Academically free in the bubble of Antioch, she perhaps thought less conventionally than some of her counterparts who attended HBCUs (historically Black colleges and universities). Her views on the Vietnam War, women's rights, and the rights of queer people were less cautious than yours. She was more radical than you. I assume this is why you loved her so passionately. However, I can only imagine, in perusing some of the letters between you two, that her challenges caused you degrees of consternation as you both tried to navigate rearing four children, your own need for personal intimacy, and a punishing public schedule. The burden fell on Cory to be the primary parent, even when she wanted to be more actively engaged in the movement as other female colleagues—Ella Baker, Dorothy Cotton, Fannie Lou Hamer, and Diane Nash—were. Tensions rose because Cory felt sidelined by motherhood. It was an impossible burden for her. You patriarchally felt that you had enough worries as it was, especially after she and Yolanda were nearly killed in Montgomery by a terrorist bombing. You both were in the thick of struggle together, which included the fight for a woman's democratic right to personal autonomy.

There is no doubt that you and Cory loved each other passionately.[21] However, there were troubling realities that you as lovers and partners faced. How open should a relationship be in perilous political times? How should you handle sex inside and outside a relationship? This was a challenge for you both, as it is for many of us. As a man, it appeared that your notion of sexuality was encased in boyish antics instead of expressions of mutuality and respect.[22] You were raised in a culture where women as sexual beings were considered subservient to men. Militarized and warrior-like, males were the aggressors, and women's consent was unimportant. In addition, the dominant culture, full of religiously informed moralism, punished sexuality even between consenting partners. Though people loved and carried on, it was deemed shameful by religious gatekeepers and state agencies, including law enforcement, who have policed Black people's perceived oversexuality since the advent of slavery. During slavery, issues of desire, desirability, intimacies, pleasure, and reproduction all centered around property ownership, and after emancipation, the "respectable" preoccupied themselves with the assumed deviancy and vice of Black sexuality. Black sexuality has been encased in mythologies that disservice Black communities and harm our self-perceptions.

This is why Bayard Rustin, an openly gay Black man, was disruptive. Rustin was charged with immorality for having sex with another man, who was White, in a Pasadena Park. Others found Rustin outrageous because he was clear about himself as a human being. His open desire of same-sex love violated religious prohibition, though it is often forgotten that he himself was a devout Quaker. Male homosexuality was taboo, more so than serial monogamy and adultery. Adam Clayton Powell Jr. threatened to tell people that you and Bayard were lovers as your national profile began to overshadow Powell's. This was quite ironic because democratic freedoms include freedoms of sexuality! Who would have believed that sex—intramarital or extramarital—would derail a movement for greater democratic rights and freedom? Yet they did and still do. Sex is still a source of extortion by the state and by individuals. This is not just peculiar to the United States; sex has been an unexamined part of society and politics across the globe. This is the terrain, intensified by your celebrity, that you and Cory navigated as marriage partners. There was nothing exotic about you or your relationship with Corey or the other women in your life, but the state wanted to stop a movement.

The other problem, as I see it, was the moralistic attitudes and contradictory behavior of Black male preachers regarding sex. Women were held publicly accountable for sexual indiscretion in many Protestant churches—especially unplanned pregnancies— but not men or male clergy or deacons. Human sexuality has been a troublesome issue for Western Christendom in general, and this became magnified among Black Protestants because of a spiritual desire to attain holiness. So we tried to live in denial of our human passions and desires. This was in a society that used our bodies to build its wealth and service its pleasures. The Black churches preached holiness but never lived it, because they expected the impossible.

Being a Black clergy member was somehow supposed to be an amulet against sex, but the truth was that it imbued you with charisma and status that was just the opposite. You were a revivalist rock star in churches filled with vulnerable men, women, and children. James Baldwin assessed in *The Fire Next Time* that many of the religious organizations were packed with Black folk full of yearnings and appetites of all sorts and repressed by societal repression and personal confusions. Powerful charismatic leaders, confused about their own issues, abused their power. This is why Malcolm X and the Honorable Elijah Muhammad fell out. Baldwin knew that between the pews were hot torrents and unfilled yearnings. These yearnings came out in a variety of ways, not always healthy. Baldwin accused religious leaders of seducing vulnerable people rather than giving them the affirmative guidance they needed. Black religious leaders, embedded in their communities, were often confused themselves about their own yearnings, and they confused their people's struggle with their own.

Ella Baker was aware of this when dealing with contradictory Black clergy members in her work with the NAACP and SCLC. Their positions were based on charisma and seductive power. Baker felt that this Black masculine clergy power was not empowering for the entire community. It notably excluded women and kept women members subservient to men within the church setting. This is the culture you grew up in and the one that shaped your masculinity. For instance, it informed who got to speak at the March on Washington. However, those inside and outside of your home questioned your perspective, and rightly so.

Freedom must be for all. Women's visibility in our communities has often been taken for granted, yet their wisdom and activism ground all democratic efforts. We rely on their persistence and need their creative resistance, though we rarely acknowledge their quest for freedom.

You knew that Black communities were composed of all types of people, and we are all kin in democratic struggle. The language of "brotherhood" and "sisterhood," borrowed from Black congregations, communicated this relatedness. We shared families, faiths, causes, and dedication to the movement. Even though the women in your life critiqued your behavior and biases, they continued to love you as their brother, father, friend, minister, son, and uncle. The women in your community were in common cause with you. They believed you had the possibility of expanding your horizons, just as you believed US society could expand its horizon.

I wish you would have lived to see the 1974 Combahee River Collective Statement.[23] The feminists who wrote that statement picked up their foremothers' democratic struggles. They were the daughters and granddaughters of those church women like your grandmother and mother.[24] They carried out their own analysis on how racism and sexism affected their communities.[25] They built upon the critique of Pauli Murray, a lawyer, legal scholar,

Episcopal priest, and cofounder of the National Organization of Women (NOW), that Jane Crow, to the same extent as Jim Crow, undermined black communities.[26] They called for solidarity with progressive Black men who understood their democratic interests were linked. The Combahee Collective called for a wider democracy. They created a document that pushed the boundaries of how we should all democratically think. They elbowed their way past the middle-class propriety that has bound our freedom struggles in chauvinistic binaries. Their democratic effort included a wide spectrum of people—low-income folks, queer and nonqueer parents, and those impoverished by all the oppressive categories that divide us. Radically, they urged that the truest content of our character is determined by how we create space for all of us to breathe. The personal is always political. It is the content of our character.

12

A STONE OF HOPE

Exactly how much will have to burn
Before we will look to the past to learn . . .
Tell me please
How many miles must we march?
—Ben Harper,
"How Many Miles Must We March"[1]

Martin,

One day in the future, the Martin Luther King Jr. Memorial in Washington, DC, might be a ruin. History is crafted from ruins. We do our best to tell the truth about the past, but we are never sure we do it full justice. What I know for certain is that you go beyond any monumental encapsulation in the nation's capital. You are a part of a living democratic tradition that arose from the bonds of enslavement and still continues in the world-historical fight to abolish oppression. The English word *freedom* is not precise. It does not fully convey the transparency we dream of, personally or societally. We seek out poets to capture what we mean when we use the word *freedom*. I love how the poet

Robert Hayden, in his poem "Frederick Douglass," articulates this freedom:

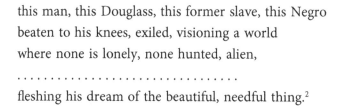

> this man, this Douglass, this former slave, this Negro
> beaten to his knees, exiled, visioning a world
> where none is lonely, none hunted, alien,
>
> . . . .
>
> fleshing his dream of the beautiful, needful thing.[2]

Hayden envisions that Douglass's life effort was to build the freedom to live without coercive greed, hatred, or violence—a freedom that is structured to enhance self-respect and community. This is the freedom tradition that has evolved over centuries.

This freedom tradition was birthed antithetically from the eighteenth-century ideology of a national republic that belonged exclusively to *White* property-holding men. In other words, an exceedingly wealthy oligarchy had ultimate say regarding who was a valuable person and a political participant.

In their own image, the constitutional framers reimagined the brutal hierarchy in ancient Greece and Rome as democracy. These ancients believed that they alone, as a city-state and as Roman citizens, were the class suited to govern. "The rest," whom they deemed barbarians and enslaved, had no right to govern them-selves. Their humanness was acknowledged only so much as it impinged upon the rights of the governing class. Anglo-Americans replicated ancient exclusivity regarding whom the republic served, belonged to, and symbolized. The sovereignty of the people did not mean all people; it meant certain people. This is how hierarchy has continuously worked in the United States.

The framers infused sacredness into the creation of the United States. Symbols of our country's inviolability are found on its most valued commodity, the dollar. Our currency depicts the great seal of the bald eagle that holds arrows representing the colonies, capped with the motto *e pluribus unum*—one from many. The opposite side of the dollar bill evidences that the country's framers thought that this new nation was conceived by divine forethought. The Eye of Providence, the biblical all-seeing eye of God, is placed atop an Egyptian pyramid, a structure that was most likely built by slave laborers. Engraved above and below the pyramidal eye are the Latin phrases *annuit cœptis*, "God has favored us," and *novus ordo seclorum*, "a new order of the ages." All who assisted in the creation of this new country wanted it to last for the ages. For them it was a predestined political body, a space where landed Anglo-Americans could live without fear of subjugation. But the United States, though crafted using sacred language, was a restricted province, not a shared one.

Private property holding morphed into to the rights of life, liberty, and the pursuit of happiness. Yet private ownership became conflated with self-autonomy in the new republic. The right of self was construed as a right belonging only to those owning private property. The new state could in effect kill the body, but it could not take away property rights. The blooming new homeland's legal sensibilities derived from England. It was a departure from monarchal sovereignty to group sovereignty. Power would be in the hands of the citizens, but the people deemed by law as citizens were White property holders.

As ingenious as the framers of the Constitution were in their protection of property-holding men, they showed little mercy or humility for those who fell outside the boundaries of their imagined new state. In Philadelphia's Independence Hall, these framers crafted varying juridical forms of disfranchisement alongside the Bill of Rights. The assurances of state protections and legal processes were only for a select few. This was not a radical departure from what other tiered societies in Africa, Asia, and Europe had done under monarchal rule and discipline. Power differentials in the new republic were racialized, which is why modern matters of democracy feel so Black and White, when they are not.

The new republic limited political participation. The powerful could voice opposition, but those who lacked social status could not. Defiant speech then was considered unruly. Unruly or not, the practice of speech was a revolutionary tool. Black spokespersons passionately honed their rhetorical skills. They summoned hope through their speeches, possessed by the word. Their voices conjured up a fuller humanity. In the beginning was the word, and words evoked hopes and dreams. Words invigorated rebellions and revolution. Words were so dangerous in the early republic that they needed to be controlled. Books were fervently banned for the enslaved and the imprisoned. Those who uttered such words of hope became piked heads on roadsides and bodies left dangling from the hangman's noose. The expression of one's conscience, one's aggravations, one's disenchantment, or one's frustration was a death knell. This need to punish dissenters was a reminder that the powerful have always been anxious and fragile. Nothing challenges them more than the spoken word. They want nothing more than silence.

However, what was even more ingenious was the way enslaved people began to divine their own humanity. Howard Thurman, one of your mentors, called these people who speak their humanity into being the "disinherited."[3] The scholar Orlando Patterson defined the loss of self-autonomy in enslavement as "natal alienation." In this process, all material possessions and progeny were stripped away and belonged to enslavers.[4] This disinheritance forced many to turn inward and ask what constitutes the self. They declared a Black humanity. The narratives they wrote described captivity in a system that sucked everything out of a person, leaving only a body that could reproduce and work. They meditated on what constituted humanity.

They hitched their philosophy to a plow and carved it out of the nearest Bible. Mahalia Jackson evokes her enslaved ancestors' journey in gospel:

> I'm on my way to Canaan Land
> I'm on my way oh to Canaan Land
> On my way Canaan Land
> On my way, glory hallelujah[5]

Canaan was utopian. This philosophical anthropology of the unlettered was a more humane vision of freedom than what was sanctioned by the politically powerful and educated elite. The driving goal of the enslaved was a fully inclusive democracy.

Today there are quite a few declension narratives regarding the unwinding of democracy. Academics and columnists alike express a foreboding about US democracy. However, for Black folk, there has always been an uneasiness with American-style democracy. Langston Hughes expressed this in the 1930s:

> There's a dream in the land
> With its back against the wall.
> By muddled names and strange
> Sometimes the dream is called.[6]

Democracies the world over are troubled. However, thinking back on the history of our country, when was democracy ever fully realized? Those who fearfully argue that democracy is unwinding miss that the three-fifths compromise was the clause of the Constitution that glued the United States together. American democracy has been troublesome and exclusive from the beginning. Modern plaintive cries over democracy's unwinding elide the realities of US history.

Mohandas Gandhi, a contradictory figure himself, understood that being democratic is fundamentally a matter of spiritual politics. This is why he had an impact on so many Black American religious leaders. "The spirit of democracy is not a mechanical thing," he wrote, "to be adjusted by abolition of forms." He observed that India's caste system and its variety of religions were barriers to the democratic spirit within India. Thus, for him, being democratic "requires a change of heart." He recognized that being democratic meant inner conversion, a changeover from the logic of domination. "I understand democracy," he opined, "as something that gives the weak the same chance as the strong." This inner conviction is the necessary spark. "Democracy must in essence, therefore, mean the art and science of mobilising," he observed. Democratic deployment requires "the entire physical, economic and spiritual resources of all the various sections of the people in the service of the common good of all."[7] This means that hand-wringing punditry might alarm us to the abuses of democracy, but it will not sustain democratic struggle.

Dismal forecasting rarely motivates people to join in struggle. Leaders always attempt to mobilize the heart. Justice struggles are not easy or swift victories. They require conviction, discipline, and faithfulness. Being democratic does not come naturally; it is a daily discipline. We all have the will to dominate. I do not say this in some ominous way. Theologians and secular social observers have long known about this aggressive behavior among our kin. This means that we must at all times be cognizant and set behavioral practices that limit our propensity to establish creeping hierarchies. Being democratic is as much a spiritual practice as it is a legal procedure.

The histories of Black Americans are instructive. Democracy has always been tenuous for us. The institutions that pundits and academics mourn have always been deadly. We have had to furiously fight to not let a destructive cancer overtake our communities. This is why you constantly conjured a better world through the spoken word. You tried to keep all of us, including yourself, from falling into fatal despair. Even when dreams turned into nightmares, you pressed forward in hope.

Sometimes, I know you felt exactly like Kendrick Lamar in "Pray for Me":

> I fight the world, I fight you, I fight myself
> I fight God, just tell me how many burdens left
> I fight pain and hurricanes, today I wept
> I'm tryna fight back tears, flood on my doorsteps[8]

Hazy spirituality cannot deny the ruthless realities of history. You were murdered by forces of the state and centuries of reinforced divisiveness. You were struck down simply because you demanded that all people be respected by law and have shared economic resources to develop their lives—the most basic elements of any democracy. This challenged society's pecking order and bred malevolence.

Democratic struggle is spiritual warfare. Its devils and demons are bureaucratic manipulation, fear, greed, jealousy, and lust. The powerful continuously downgrade the expectation that society can balance competing interests. Monarchical power, monopoly, is always their cop-out. Their never-ending quest for supremacy will only be complete when the masses are forced to crown a royal. Organizing and resistance require more than catchphrases. They require an armament of hope. This is why your sermons often had a heart-stirring crescendo. Hope buoys and fortifies the heart. It is no surprise that former president Barack Obama paraphrased your idea of audacity as a spiritual assertion of one's own self-worth. "But despite the existence of a system that denies our essential worth," you stated, "we must have the spiritual audacity to assert our somebodiness."[9] Obama's *The Audacity of Hope*, a book written in 2006 that previews his 2008 campaign, took the jagged edges off your understanding that a spiritual boldness was required to mobilize and generate social change.[10]

Hope is vital to endure the pains of struggle. No one can exist in the weary day-in, day-out grind of life without some kind of hope. So our ancestors radically dreamed. They often sought otherworldly solutions to worldly problems because they held onto hope in a sea of despair. These spiritual sages of freedom, many of whom lived in perpetual bondage, imagined how to exist beyond the confinement of the fields as they sang:

> I got shoes, you got shoes,
> All God's children got shoes.
> When I get to Heav'n gonna put on my shoes,
> Gonna walk all over God's Heav'n, Heav'n, Heav'n[11]

Hope then is as much a necessity as social analysis is. The skills to examine the contradictions within our past are important, but so is the spiritual capacity see beyond everyday sameness. No social movement has been enacted without hope. This is where academics, journalists, and pundits are constantly misled. They believe their ability to analyze a condition is truer to people's understanding than the spirit is. What made you dangerous was that you attempted, however imperfectly, to be an honest broker of the people's hopes.

Writer Ta-Nehisi Coates has a more pessimistic take on the world than I have been suggesting. His brilliantly crafted *Between the World and Me* is a realistic meditation about the fears and despairs that modern Black people endure. Contemporary politics can be scornful and filled with unrepentant greed. I, too, worry about my children's and grandchildren's fate. However, I cannot think of a time when scorn has not been heaped upon Black humanity. Nor can I think of a time when this same humanity did not counterpunch a sneering society with a spirituality grounded in the hope of a livable future.

In Howard Thurman's memoir, *With Head and Heart*, his illiterate grandmother, who was born into slavery, heard a word of hope from an enslaved preacher. Thurman writes:

> Once or twice a year, the slave master would permit a slave preacher from a neighboring plantation to come over to preach to his slaves. The slave preacher followed a long tradition, which has hovered over the style of certain black preachers even to present time. It is to bring the sermon to a grand climax by a dramatization of the crucifixion and resurrection of Jesus. . . . At the end, he would be exhausted, but his congregation would be uplifted and sustained with courage to withstand the difficulties of the week to come. When the slave preacher told the Calvary narrative to my grandmother and the other slaves, it had the same effect on them as it would later have on their descendants. But this preacher, when he had finished, would pause, his eyes scrutinizing every face in the congregation, and then he would tell them, "You are not niggers! You are not slaves! You are God's children!"[12]

Thurman notes that his grandmother told her grandchildren that story to give them the courage to continue. "When she had finished, our spirits were restored," he penned.[13] So while I admire Coates's eloquent prose, I found his brutally honest description unsatisfactory to maintain a spiritually informed democratic struggle. Coates, following a lineage of democratic free thinkers, writes with an agnostic approach. But when has philosophy alone been consequential to resistance and community building? One constant in the histories of Black Americans has been hope. This is how the ancestors lived through the barbarities of enslavement to keep their humanity intact. Where lies the hope in his reflections to his son? Where is the restoration of the spirit that keeps our struggles from veering off toward xenophobia and hatred?

The building of democracy requires a spirit. Du Bois reflected on this in *The Souls of Black Folk*, his collection of essays that in part tried to replace what Du Bois believed was the crudity of rural Black religion with the "kingdom of culture." He wrote, "This, then, is the end of striving: to be a co-worker in the kingdom of culture, to escape both death and isolation, to husband and use his best powers and his latent genius."[14] Du Bois's idea of the kingdom of culture was his secularized substitute for the Calvinist doctrines of the Heidelberg Catechism that asked, "What is our only hope in life and death?" and the Westminster Shorter Catechism that asked, "What is the chief end of man?" The answer: "to love and serve God." Du Bois, "like his peers and mentors, was in a transition from a theological vocation of the intellectual to teach and search for truth, toward what he believed to be a broader and more intellectually consistent basis for inclusion of all humanity. The highest good for human beings was to be 'co-workers in the kingdom of culture,' and all people played a role in building this kingdom."[15] This "kingdom," however, could not replace the

strength that those same rural Black people found with preachers and spiritual enablers. They proved to be more empowering
than the idea of the kingdom of culture. And it was in the very
practice of running their own institutions that Black folk learned
a collective spirit of democracy.

I am empathetic toward Coates's spiritual disinclinations just
as I understand Du Bois's tendency toward secularity. However,
democracy has a spiritual history that must be reckoned with
too. For many Black people, this history evolved from their own
collective fashionings, where all their hopes and utopian imaginings mixed with a fervent religiosity. They formed their own
discursive communities—churches, clubs, mosques, temples—in
which they debated their most mundane and sacred concerns. The
communities they built were democratic in the sense that they
allowed for different viewpoints on the world to be expressed.
These pluralistic communities embodied their hopes more so than
the atomistic philosophies underlying so much of contemporary
social critique. These institutions that housed Black spiritualities
were foundational to both collective and individual freedom.

Hopes are often dashed, and dreams go unfulfilled. In a sermon titled "Shattered Dreams"—your countermelody to Langston
Hughes's poem "Harlem"—you preached to your congregants at
Dexter Avenue Baptist Church as though you were preaching to
yourself. You advised Dexter's congregants to face disappointment
by finding infinite hope. Infinite hope, you said, was how our
enslaved ancestors lived beyond chattel existence. You made your
congregants' hearts sing as you summarized their overcoming of
these setbacks:

> In the final analysis our ability to deal creatively with shat-
> tered dreams and blasted hopes will be determined by the
> extent of our faith in God. A genuine faith will imbue us

with the conviction that there is a God beyond time and a Life beyond Life. Thus we know that we are not alone in any circumstance, however dismal and catastrophic it may be. God dwells with us in life's confining and oppressive cells. And even if we die there having not received the earthly promise, he will walk with us down that mysterious road called death, and lead us at last to that indescribable city that he has prepared for us. Let us never feel that God's creative power is exhausted by this earthly life, and his majestic love is locked within the limited walls of time and space. This would be a strongly irrational universe if God did not bring about an ultimate wedding of virtue and fulfillment.[16]

Today, like Coates, many Generation X and millennials do not hold onto communal faith in the way you did with your congregants over sixty years ago. However, to endure, all of us must minimally find some community to build our hopes with. Hopes inform our human decency. Hopes help us to construct our collective dreams and personal imaginings. They can be our ethical guideposts. You steadfastly preached the relevancy of hope. Hope is critical to social analysis of the world's cruelties. Hope is an antibody to misanthropic cancer. "Keep hope alive" is the refrain of your mentee Jesse Jackson Sr.

Hope is gathered from the ruins. We gather it from the fragments. Most enslaved people did not know who Toussaint Louverture was, but they understood his struggle in leading a people against forced labor and total coercion. They knew he was heroic. And his heroism extended far beyond his small island of Haiti or his Parisian prison cell.

Black leaders who traveled to India did not fully appreciate the intricacies of Indian politics, Gandhi's problems, or the Dalits' struggles. What they understood, though, was that a dark brown

man led his people in a freedom struggle against English imperialism. The Chinese student who wore the banner WE SHALL
OVERCOME in Tiananmen Square in 1989 probably never met
any African Americans or understood the ideological divides of
the civil rights movement. But he understood that the song of
freedom empowers people to act collectively. Hope must always
be kept alive, as it is the core of any democracy.

Yes, one day your statue that stands majestically in Washington,
DC, which so many fought to see erected, may be a ruin. But
democracy will never be a ruin. People will come near and far
to collect those stones. Some will save them as amulets. Others
will sling them as if in the intifada, David versus Goliath. Some
will pick them up and hold them as keepsakes for their children
and grandchildren. This is why you reminded the Black people
gathered at the Holt Street Baptist Church in Montgomery in 1955
that they embodied hope. The spirit of the times did not just pull
you along but also carried those occupying the pews that fateful
night, and you believed they had a mission. You charged them to
recognize the propitious moment:

> There lived a race of people, a *black* people, "fleecy locks
> and black complexion," a people who had the moral cour-
> age to stand up for their rights. And thereby they injected a
> new meaning into the veins of history and of civilization.[17]

The New Testament passage in Hebrews 11:1 (NRSV) was
always a reminder to you of what faith is all about: "Now faith
is the assurance of things hoped for, the conviction of things not
seen." You translated it with powerful conviction: "With this faith,
we will be able to hew out of the mountain of despair a stone of
hope."[18] This is the foundation of democracy.

EPILOGUE

Picket lines and picket signs
Don't punish me with brutality
Talk to me, so you can see
Oh, what's going on
—MARVIN GAYE, "WHAT'S GOING ON"[1]

Martin,

In 2016 the election of Donald Trump set the intellectual world's hair on fire. But Trump was never the sole problem. His most grotesque moments mirror the grotesqueness of US history, a democracy built on slave labor, a privileged society that exists for a few, not for all. This is particularly true for the White oligarchical class and those who aspire to be in it. This class's great fear is the loss of its dominance. The old dominant class in the first half of the twentieth century, the Protestant establishment, used anti-Catholicism and anti-Semitism to rule. However, even more so they used anti-Blackness. They feared Blackness not because of race but because of its revolutionary potential to challenge their ruling authority. They attempted to keep Black and Indigenous people as childlike wards of the state. And worse, they framed people of color as a detestable stain on their White republic. Yet the very wealthiest had limits placed on them. They were held accountable by a Protestant morality, even with its shortcomings. This morality is represented by the churches that still stand on every corner of big cities and in town squares. It was understood at that time that even the rich had to account to a God and had moral responsibility and shame.

These churches did not mean the ruling classes were truly guided by the proposition that there was a just God who equally judged all people. If that were the case, racial pogroms—including the terrorism of lynchings—that were carried out in God's name would never have occurred. Nevertheless, because these churches stood on the corner, they represented an institutional possibility that a just society, democratic and inclusive, was possible. Members of Protestant sects coming out of England, Holland, and Scotland were dissenters from the English and Roman Catholic monopolies on their spiritual aspirations. English dissenters used the imperial lanes opened to them by their monarchy's coercive might and convinced themselves that, by coming to North America, they might fulfill their spiritual quest for a land of their own. They, however, ignored that there were people who preexisted them, who also held spiritual aspirations and dreams. The colonists conquered the inhabitants and then ignominiously excluded Indigenous people's dreams and faiths. The invaders built incomplete democratic institutions using their Baptist, Congregational, Presbyterian, and Quaker governance—which still root our democracy today.

Long before Jürgen Habermas, the Frankfurt School political philosopher, began discussing communicative action, these religious institutions were scenes of debate and deliberation locally and globally.[2] These discussions were the theoretical basis of US constitutionalism. Black leaders, including you, from enslavement to the present used the moral basis of Protestantism to challenge forms of social exclusion. These histories are what your mobilizing preaching drew upon.

Martin, you spoke in the democratic language of faith that came from your Baptist heritage. This is one of the reasons your voice was socially resonant. Every freedom struggle has to speak in a language that makes sense to people in their times. The zeitgeist of the 1950s, the zenith of US church attendance, allowed you to be a defining voice in the collective effort to transform US democracy.[3] You arrived on the scene when many US citizens continued to hold an idealistic narrative of the country's founding—one without enslavement, legalized exclusions, or attempted genocides. In 1955 a vision of a beloved community, a moral sensibility guiding democratic politics, made sense. After all, many wealthy religious and nonreligious types used this same narrative to create the illusion of the US as a God-fearing nation in opposition to the godlessness of communism.

Times changed. Humorist Jean Shepherd's 1966 novel *In God We Trust: All Others Pay Cash*, which is made up of fictionalized accounts of his life in Hammond, Indiana, sums up our current sentiments. "It's all about the Benjamins," as hip-hop producer P. Diddy rapped in 1997. Members of the White male Anglo-Saxon Protestant establishment that once ruled the country were as unsentimental about money and power as today's godless capitalists. What is arguably different from today's ultrarich is that members of the old establishment wore the mask of being God-fearing and held onto minimal standards of respectability. This limited chivalry ended by the 1980s. From then on, our world turned on its axis through hierarchy and power determined by control of algorithms. Technological dominance, or "thingification" as you warily warned, became a new reality.

Martin, when you hitched yourself to that grand mobilization in Montgomery, newly independent states in Africa and Asia were buoyed by the struggle being waged in the former capital of the old Confederacy. Back in 1958 you optimistically believed a new world was being birthed:

> Those of us who live in the Twentieth Century are privileged to live in one of the most momentous periods of human history. It is an exciting age filled with hope. It is an age in which a new social order is being born. We stand today between two worlds—the dying old and the emerging new.[4]

In the United States, many hoped they could right the world with a sense of justice. Throughout the twentieth century, there were two senseless world wars. The second contained ghastly horrors—Nazi concentration camps, the Nanjing Massacre, Soviet gulags, and the bombings of Hiroshima and Nagasaki. There was utter cynicism and despair around the globe. Faith of a kind was needed. For thirteen years, from 1955 to 1968, you and your collaborating freedom fighters exuded a full-throated democratic faith. That faith gave you the strength to love and the political fortitude to wage a relentless jihad against antidemocratic behavior. "In God we trust" and "Thus sayeth the Lord!" was the language of the time. However, today there is not much faith, not even coming from those religious houses who project themselves to be the most pious.

At this historical juncture, we are in battle with godless capitalists, whether private oligarchs or state-controlled ones. They have faith only in materiality. They do not value giving voice, and they determinedly wish to thwart democracy and demand conformity. To them, this has become a more efficient way of maintaining power, more so than governing through consent. The values of equity, fairness, deliberation, and respect are sacrificed on the altar of avarice. We are in an expanded global struggle. Today all around the world, we are faced with a heated planet resulting in daily weather catastrophes in addition to multitudinous "isms" we have and must fight against. Today more than ever, being democratic is a challenge. Today more than ever, we must meditate on what it means to manifest democracy as an inner directiveness, as a way of living in a world of parties seeking dominance over their vulnerable populations.

To consciously live democratically we must have an abiding faith that democracy is worth struggling to maintain—not just for ourselves but for all people. This is what you taught us. Being democratic means that no matter the persuasion or the disposition or the inclination, persons deserve to be heard, listened to, respected, and cared for. Our purpose on this habitable garden is to provide oxygen and hydration so that all of us can flourish. This, then, is the ultimate aim of our democratic struggles: a garden to breathe in and to roam through for all of us. This is the essence of spirituality.

This requires us to go beyond materialism. Enshrined power is always perceived as unalterable. And all of us are always prey to powerful idols, capitalist or otherwise. Yet at the heart of all divinity is a deeper sense of our commonalities. This is the spirituality that democracy is built upon. This is the spirituality that must guide our political stances and personal lives. We must be continuously dedicated in our efforts to build democratic institutions. For it is within these institutions that our hopes are shaped into realities. Democratic spaces allow our fears about newcomers and those who are different to find factual adjudication. Each one of us, as individuals and in our collectives, must search for some ultimate goodness that sustains the sanctity of our lives together. We must internalize the spirit of democracy. Without this spirit, as you repeatedly warned us, we face a dicey future at best. In

your "Beyond Vietnam" speech at Riverside Church in April of
1967, you warned the country that even the greatest of nations
are destroyed by hubris. We would do well to heed your words:

> We are now faced with the fact, my friends, that tomorrow is
> today. . . . Over the bleached bones and jumbled residues of
> numerous civilizations are written the pathetic words, "Too
> late." There is an invisible book of life that faithfully records
> our vigilance or our neglect. Omar Khayyam is right: "The
> moving finger writes, and having writ moves on."[5]

ACKNOWLEDGMENTS

Writing is solitary but not books in publication. I want to thank my literary agent Sha-Shana Crichton, Esq., who passionately believed in this project. Thanks to all the staff at Chicago Review Press, especially senior acquisitions editor Jerome Pohlen and assistant project editor Frances Giguette. Thanks goes to my University of Michigan classmate and friend Diane Proctor Reeder, who first read the entire manuscript critically—Go Blue! Thanks goes to Dr. Clayborne Carson, whose tireless drive built the Stanford University Martin Luther King Jr. Research and Education Institute and the King Papers project, and Dr. Vicki Crawford, director of the Morehouse College Martin Luther King Jr. Collection. These collections, available online and physically, provided rich access to the primary materials I needed. I would be remiss not to thank all the great scholars who have written on Martin Luther King Jr. I also want to thank my University of Kansas African American Studies and American Studies undergraduate and graduate students, who sat through my seminar on Martin Luther King Jr. and provided me with great insight. I would not have written this book if were not for the Reverend H. Scott Matheney of Elmhurst College and his invitation to speak on MLK Day in 2017. That invitation set my imagination ablaze and this book in motion. I would also like to thank the staff at Emporia State University, who invited me to share my thoughts on King, and the great staff at the Gerald R. Ford Presidential Museum in Grand Rapids, Michigan, who invited me to share portions of what is written in this book before the world shut down in 2020. Thanks goes to Dr. Danielle Allen, Gerald Early, Jonathan Eig, Dr. Serene Jones, Dr. Melanye Price, and Dr. Heather Richardson for endorsing this book in rough draft—I am eternally grateful. Then there is family. I want to thank my loving family and friends, who allowed me to be grumpy, randomly talk to myself, and have space as I tried to figure out what I felt compelled to say via these pages.

NOTES

Prologue

1. "Winter in America," Gil Scott-Heron and Brian Jackson, track 7 on *Midnight Band: The First Minute of a New Day*, Arista, 1975.
2. Vincent Harding, *There Is a River: The Black Struggle for Freedom in America* (New York: Harcourt Brace Jovanovich, 1981).
3. "Ella's Song," Sweet Honey in the Rock, by Bernice Johnson Reagon, track 2 on *Breaths*, Flying Fish Records, 1988.
4. Howard Thurman, *Footprints of a Dream: The Story of the Church for the Fellowship of All Peoples* (Eugene, OR: Wipf and Stock, 2009), 7.

1. Network of Mutuality

1. "Wake Up Everybody," Harold Melvin & The Blue Notes, by Victor Carstarphen, Gene McFadden, John Whitehead, track 1 on *Wake Up Everybody*, Philadelphia International, 1975.
2. Jonathan Rieder, *The Word of the Lord Is upon Me: The Righteous Performance of Martin Luther King, Jr.* (Cambridge, MA: Harvard University Press, 2010).
3. Martin Luther King Jr., "King in 1967: 'My Dream Has Turned into a Nightmare,'" interview by Sander Vanocur, NBC News, May 8, 1967, https://www.nbcnews.com/nightly-news/king-1967-my-dream-has -turned-nightmare-flna8C11013179.
4. Kevin M. Kruse, *One Nation Under God: How Corporate America Invented Christian America* (New York: Basic Books, 2015).
5. Cedric J. Robinson, *Black Movements in America* (New York: Routledge, 2013).

6. Martin Luther King Jr., "Remaining Awake Through a Great Revolution," in *A Knock at Midnight: Inspiration from the Great Sermons of Reverend Martin Luther King, Jr.*, Clayborne Carson and Peter Holloran, eds. (New York: Warner Books, 1998), accessed via https://kinginstitute.stanford .edu/king-papers/publications/knock-midnight-inspiration-great -sermons-reverend-martin-luther-king-jr-10.

7. Elesha Coffman, "What Luther Said," *Christian History*, August 8, 2008, https://www.christianitytoday.com/history/2008/august/what-luther -said.html.

8. Katie Wedell et al., "George Floyd Is Not Alone. 'I Can't Breathe Uttered by Dozens in Fatal Police Holds Across US," *USA Today*, June 25, 2020, https://www.usatoday.com/in-depth/news/investigations/2020/06/13 /george-floyd-not-alone-dozens-said-cant-breathe-police-holds/3137 373001/.

9. Orlando Patterson, *Freedom*, vol. 1, *Freedom in the Making of Western Culture* (New York: Basic Books, 1991).

10. Steven Levitsky and Daniel Ziblatt, *How Democracies Die* (New York: Crown, 2018); Nancy MacLean, *Democracy in Chains: The Deep History of the Radical Right's Stealth Plan for America* (New York: Scribe, 2017); George Packer, *The Unwinding: An Inner History of the New America* (New York: Macmillan, 2013).

11. James T. Kloppenberg, *Toward Democracy: The Struggle for Self-Rule in European and American Thought* (New York: Oxford University Press, 2016).

12. Patterson, *Freedom*, vol. 1; Edmund S. Morgan, *American Slavery, American Freedom* (New York: W. W. Norton, 2003); Howard Thurman, *Deep River and the Negro Speaks of Life and Death* (Richmond, Indiana: Friends United Press, 1975).

13. King, "Remaining Awake."

2. The Highest Ethical Ideal

1. Odetta, "Spiritual Trilogy: 'Oh, Freedom,' 'Come and Go with Me,' 'I'm on My Way,'" track 16 on *Odetta Sings Ballads and Blues*, Tradition, 1956.

2. Martin Luther King Jr., "Letter from Birmingham Jail," accessed via Martin Luther King, Jr., Research and Education Institute, Stanford University, https://kinginstitute.stanford.edu/king-papers/documents/letter -birmingham-jail.

3. Martin Luther King Jr., "Address at the Conclusion of the Selma to Montgomery March," March 25, 1965, accessed via Martin Luther King, Jr., Research and Education Institute, Stanford University, https://king institute.stanford.edu/king-papers/documents/address-conclusion -selma-montgomery-march.

4. Langston Hughes, "Let America Be America Again," accessed via the Poetry Foundation, https://poets.org/poem/let-america-be-america-again.

5. Martin Luther King Jr., "I Have a Dream," speech on August 28, 1963, at the March on Washington for Jobs and Freedom, accessed via Martin Luther King, Jr., Research and Education Institute, Stanford University, https:// kinginstitute.stanford.edu/king-papers/documents/i-have-dream -address-delivered-march-washington-jobs-and-freedom.

6. Martin Luther King Jr., "MIA Mass Meeting at Holt Street Baptist Church," speech given on December 5, 1955, in Montgomery, Alabama, accessed via Martin Luther King, Jr., Research and Education Institute, Stanford University, https://kinginstitute.stanford.edu/king-papers/documents/mia-mass -meeting-holt-street-baptist-church.

7. J. Morgan Kousser, *The Shaping of Southern Politics: Suffrage Restriction and the Establishment of the One-Party South* (New Haven, CT: Yale University Press, 1974).

8. Gavin Wright, *Sharing the Prize: The Economics of the Civil Rights Revolution in the American South* (Cambridge, MA: Harvard University Press, 2018).

9. James T. Kloppenberg, *Toward Democracy: The Struggle for Self-Rule in European and American Thought* (New York: Oxford University Press, 2016).

10. Graham Burchell, Colin Gordon, and Peter Miller, eds., *The Foucault Effect: Studies in Governmentality* (Chicago: University of Chicago Press, 1991).

11. J. G. A. Pocock, *The Machiavellian Moment: Florentine Political Thought and the Atlantic Republican Tradition*, rev. ed. (Princeton, NJ: Princeton University Press, 2016).

12. Richard Wright, *The Color Curtain: A Report on the Bandung Conference* (Oxford, Mississippi: University Press of Mississippi, 1995).

13. Martin Luther King Jr., *"In a Single Garment of Destiny": A Global Vision of Justice*, ed. Lewis Baldwin (Boston: Beacon Press, 2013).

14. Francis Fukuyama, *The End of History and the Last Man* (New York: Free Press, 1992).

15. Martin Luther King Jr., "Beyond Vietnam," April 4, 1967, speech at Riverside Church, New York City, accessed via Martin Luther King, Jr., Research and Education Institute, Stanford University, https://kinginstitute .stanford.edu/king-papers/documents/beyond-vietnam.
16. Martin Luther King Jr., *Why We Can't Wait* (New York: Harper & Row, 1964).
17. Martin Luther King Jr., "Our God Is Marching On!" speech on March 25, 1965, Montgomery, Alabama, accessed via Martin Luther King, Jr., Research and Education Institute, Stanford University, https://kinginstitute .stanford.edu/our-god-marching.

3. A Revolution of Values

1. Martin Luther King Jr., *Where Do We Go from Here: Chaos or Community?* (Boston: Beacon Press, 1967), 196.
2. Martin Luther King Jr., "Beyond Vietnam," April 4, 1967, speech at Riverside Church, New York City, accessed via Martin Luther King, Jr., Research and Education Institute, Stanford University, https://kinginstitute .stanford.edu/king-papers/documents/beyond-vietnam.
3. Sam Fleischacker, "Economics and the Ordinary Person: Re-reading Adam Smith," The Library of Economics and Liberty, October 4, 2004, https:// www.econlib.org/library/Columns/y2004/FleischackerSmith.html.
4. Jennifer Burns, *Goddess of the Market: Ayn Rand and the American Right* (New York: Oxford University Press, 2009).
5. King, *Where Do We Go,* 196.
6. Martin Luther King Jr., "I Have a Dream," speech on August 28, 1963, at the March on Washington for Jobs and Freedom, accessed via Martin Luther King, Jr., Research and Education Institute, Stanford University, https:// kinginstitute.stanford.edu/king-papers/documents/i-have-dream -address-delivered-march-washington-jobs-and-freedom.
7. Martin Luther King Jr., "I've Been to the Mountaintop," speech on April 3, 1968, at Bishop Charles Mason Temple, Memphis, Tennessee, accessed via Martin Luther King, Jr., Research and Education Institute, Stanford University, https://kinginstitute.stanford.edu/encyclopedia/ive-been-mountain top?wpmm=1&wpisrc=nl_daily202.
8. Kellie Carter Jackson, *Force and Freedom: Black Abolitionists and the Politics of Violence* (Philadelphia: University of Pennsylvania Press, 2019).

9. King, *Where Do We Go*, 57.

10. King, 65

11. King, "Beyond Vietnam."

12. King, "Beyond Vietnam."

13. Martin Luther King Jr., "A Comparison of the Conceptions of God in the Thinking of Paul Tillich and Henry Nelson Wieman," in *The Papers of Martin Luther King, Jr.*, eds. Clayborne Carson et al., vol. 2, *Rediscovering Precious Values, July 1951–November 1955* (Berkley, CA: University of California Press, 1994).

14. Henry David Thoreau, "Economy," in *Walden* (Cambridge: Riverside Press, 1906), 8–9, https://www.walden.org/work/walden/.

15. Martin Luther King Jr., "MLK—A Riot Is the Language of the Unheard," interview by Mike Wallace, *60 Minutes*, CBS, September 27, 1966, https://www.youtube.com/watch?v=_K0BWXjJv5s.

16. "Ella's Song," Sweet Honey in the Rock, by Bernice Johnson Reagon, track 2 on *Breaths*, Flying Fish Records, 1988.

17. Martin Luther King Jr., "The Birth of a New Age," speech on August 11, 1956, at Alpha Phi Alpha, Buffalo, New York, accessed via Martin Luther King, Jr., Research and Education Institute, Stanford University, https://kinginstitute.stanford.edu/king-papers/documents/birth-new-age-address-delivered-11-august-1956-fiftieth-anniversary-alpha-phi.

4. Like a King

1. Ben Harper, "Like a King," track 8 on *Welcome to the Cruel World*, Virgin, 1994.

2. Otis Spann with Muddy Waters and His Band, "Tribute to Martin Luther King," track 3 on *Live the Life*, Testament, 1968.

3. Nina Simone, "Why? (The King of Love is Dead)," by Gene Taylor, track 6 on *'Nuff Said!* RCA Victor, 1968.

4. Dion, "Abraham, Martin and John," by Dick Holler, track 1 on *Dion*, Laurie Records, 1968.

5. Nancy Dupree, "Docta King," track 4 on *Ghetto Reality*, Folkways Records, 1969.

6. "R&B Legend Stevie Wonder's Role in Making Martin Luther King Jr. Day a National Holiday," National Museum of African American Music,

January 10, 2019, https://nmaam.org/2019/01/10/rb-legend-stevie-wonders
-role-making-martin-luther-king-jr-day-national-holiday/.

7. Stevie Wonder, "Happy Birthday," track 5 on side 2 of *Hotter than July*,
Tamla, 1980.

8. Public Enemy, "By the Time I Get to Arizona," track 7 on *Apocalypse 91. . . The Enemy Strikes Back*, Def Jam, 1991.

9. Martin Luther King Jr., "I've Been to the Mountaintop," speech on April 3,
1968, at Bishop Charles Mason Temple, Memphis, Tennessee, accessed via
Martin Luther King, Jr., Research and Education Institute, Stanford University, https://kinginstitute.stanford.edu/encyclopedia/ive-been-mountain
top?wpmm=1&wpisrc=nl_daily202.

10. Martin Luther King Jr., "I Have a Dream," speech on August 28, 1963,
at the March on Washington for Jobs and Freedom, accessed via Martin
Luther King, Jr., Research and Education Institute, Stanford University,
https://kinginstitute.stanford.edu/king-papers/documents/i-have
-dream-address-delivered-march-washington-jobs-and-freedom.

11. Robin D. G. Kelley, "The Riddle of the Zoot: Malcolm Little and Black
Cultural Politics during World War II," in *Race and the Subject of Masculin-
ities*, eds. Harry Stecopoulos and Michael Uebel (London: Duke University
Press, 1997), 231–252, https://doi.org/10.1215/9780822397748-009.

12. Julius Lester, "The Angry Children of Malcolm X," *Sing Out!* 16 (October/
November 1966): 21–25, https://www.crmvet.org/info/661100_lester
_children_of.pdf.

13. The literature comparing King and X is now voluminous. Most recently,
see Peniel E. Joseph's *The Sword and the Shield: The Revolutionary Lives
of Malcolm X and Martin Luther King Jr.* (New York: Basic Books, 2020).

14. Martin Luther King Jr., "Next Stop: The North," *Saturday Review*, November 13, 1965, 34.

15. Charles Johnson, *Dreamer: A Novel* (New York: Simon and Schuster,
1998), 160.

16. "Clouter with Conscience," *Time,* March 15, 1963, 26.

17. Cecil Adams, "What's the Origin of 'the City That Works'?" *Chicago Reader*,
September 3, 2009, https://web.archive.org/web/20170419202705/http://
chicago.straightdope.com/sdc20090903.php.

18. Johnson, *Dreamer*, 218–219.

19. Martin Luther King Jr., "Why Jesus Called a Man a Fool," August 27, 1967, speech delivered at the Mount Pisgah Baptist Church in Chicago, accessed via Martin Luther King, Jr., Research and Education Institute, Stanford University, https://kinginstitute.stanford.edu/king-papers /documents/why-jesus-called-man-fool-sermon-delivered-mount -pisgah-missionary-baptist.

20. Johnson, *Dreamer*, 138–140.

21. Martin Luther King Jr., "Science Surpasses the Social Order," in *The Papers of Martin Luther King, Jr.*, eds. Clayborne Carson et al., vol. 6, *Advocate of the Social Gospel, September 1948–March 1963* (Berkeley, CA: University of California Press, 2007).

5. Drum Major Instinct

1. Martin Luther King Jr., "The Drum Major Instinct," speech on February 4, 1968, at Ebenezer Baptist Church, accessed via Martin Luther King, Jr., Research and Education Institute, Stanford University, https://king institute.stanford.edu/king-papers/documents/drum-major-instinct -sermon-delivered-ebenezer-baptist-church.

2. "West, Obama, and King's Bible," *Tavis Smiley Presents*, C-SPAN, January 17, 2013, https://www.c-span.org/video/?c4474015/user-clip-west -obama-kings-bible.

3. Barack Obama, "Remarks by the President at the Acceptance of the Nobel Peace Prize," December 10, 2009, The White House, President Barack Obama, https://obamawhitehouse.archives.gov/the-press-office /remarks-president-acceptance-nobel-peace-prize.

4. Saul D. Alinsky, *Rules for Radicals: A Practical Primer for Realistic Radicals* (New York: Vintage, 1989).

5. Elizabeth Alexander, *The Black Interior: Essays* (Minneapolis: Graywolf Press, 2004).

6. Howard Thurman, *The Inward Journey* (Richmond, Indiana: Friends United Press, 2007).

7. Ralph E. Luker, "Johns the Baptist," *RalphLuker.com* (blog), http://www .ralphluker.com/vjohns/baptist.html.

8. Houston Bryan Roberson, *Fighting the Good Fight: The Story of the Dexter Avenue King Memorial Baptist Church, 1865–1977* (New York: Routledge, 2005); Ralph E. Luker, "Murder and Biblical Memory: The Legend

of Vernon Johns," *The Virginia Magazine of History and Biography* 112, no. 4 (2004): 372–418, accessed August 11, 2021, http://www.jstor.org /stable/4250212.

9. Samuel Momodu, "Baton Rouge Bus Boycott (1953)," Black Past, https:// www.blackpast.org/african-american-history/events-african-american -history/baton-rouge-bus-boycott-1953/.

10. Thomas Shepherd, "Must Jesus Bear the Cross Alone," 1693, Timeless Truths, https://library.timelesstruths.org/music/Must_Jesus_Bear_the_Cross _Alone/.

11. David Garrow, *Bearing the Cross: Martin Luther King Jr. and the Southern Leadership Conference* (New York: W. Morrow, 1986).

12. George Bennard, "The Old Rugged Cross," 1912, https://www.hymnal .net/en/hymn/h/618.

13. Vincent Harding, *Martin Luther King: The Inconvenient Hero* (Maryknoll, New York: Orbis Books, 1996).

14. Mahalia Jackson, vocalist, "Move On Up a Little Higher," by W. Hebert Brewster, Apollo, 1947; Robert F. Darden, "'Move On Up Little Higher'— Mahalia Jackson (1947)," Library of Congress, http://www.loc.gov/static /programs/national-recording-preservation-board/documents/MoveOn UpALittleHigher.pdf.

6. The Strength to Love

1. U2, "Pride (In the Name of Love)," track 2 on *The Unforgettable Fire*, CBS Ireland, 1984.

2. Martha C. Nussbaum, chap. 10 in *Political Emotions: Why Love Matters for Justice* (Cambridge, MA: Harvard University Press, 2013).

3. Martin Luther King Jr., "I Have a Dream," speech on August 28, 1963, at the March on Washington for Jobs and Freedom, accessed via Martin Luther King, Jr., Research and Education Institute, Stanford University, https:// kinginstitute.stanford.edu/king-papers/documents/i-have-dream -address-delivered-march-washington-jobs-and-freedom.

4. "Jesus Paid It All," lyrics by Elvina M. Hall, 1865, https://hymnary.org /text/i_hear_the_savior_say_thy_strength_indee.

5. Martin Luther King Jr., "MIA Mass Meeting at Holt Street Baptist Church," speech given on December 5, 1955, in Montgomery, Alabama, accessed via

Martin Luther King, Jr., Research and Education Institute, Stanford University, https://kinginstitute.stanford.edu/king-papers/documents/mia-mass-meeting-holt-street-baptist-church.

6. W. E. B. Du Bois, *Black Reconstruction in America: Toward a History of the Part Which Black Folk Played in the Attempt to Reconstruct Democracy in America, 1860–1880* (New York: Harcourt, Brace & Company, 1935).

7. Matt. 22:34–40 (New Revised Standard Version).

8. Orlando Patterson, *Ethnic Chauvinism: The Reactionary Impulse* (New York: Stein and Day, 1977).

9. Martin Luther King Jr., "The Significant Contribution of Jeremiah to Religious Thought," in *The Papers of Martin Luther King, Jr.*, eds. Clayborne Carson, Ralph Luker, and Penny A. Russell, vol. 1, *Called to Serve, January 1929–June 1951* (Berkeley, CA: University of California Press, 1992).

10. Reggie Williams, *Bonhoeffer's Black Jesus: Harlem Renaissance Theology and an Ethic of Resistance* (Waco, TX: Baylor University Press, 2014).

11. Martin Luther King Jr., "Martin Luther King Jr. Saw Three Evils in the World," *The Atlantic Monthly*, King Issue, 2018, https://www.theatlantic.com/magazine/archive/2018/02/martin-luther-king-hungry-club-forum/552533/.

12. Martin Luther King Jr., "I've Been to the Mountaintop," speech on April 3, 1968, at Bishop Charles Mason Temple, Memphis, Tennessee, accessed via Martin Luther King, Jr., Research and Education Institute, Stanford University, https://kinginstitute.stanford.edu/encyclopedia/ive-been-mountaintop?wpmm=1&wpisrc=nl_daily202.

13. Jonathan Rieder, *The Word of the Lord Is upon Me: The Righteous Performance of Martin Luther King, Jr.* (Cambridge, MA: Harvard University Press, 2010).

14. Stephen L. Carter, *Civility: Manners, Morals, and the Etiquette of Democracy* (New York: Basic Books, 1998).

15. Danielle Allen, *Talking to Strangers: Anxieties of Citizenship Since Brown v. Board of Education* (Chicago: University of Chicago Press, 2004).

16. Martin Luther King Jr., "Give Us the Ballot," speech on May 17, 1957, at the Prayer Pilgrimage for Freedom, Washington, DC, accessed via Martin Luther King, Jr., Research and Education Institute, Stanford University, https://kinginstitute.stanford.edu/king-papers/documents/give-us-ballot-address-delivered-prayer-pilgrimage-freedom.

17. "Violent Crime Control and Law Enforcement Act of 1994," H.R. 3355, 103rd Cong., 1993–1994, https://www.congress.gov/bill/103rd-congress /house-bill/3355/text.

7. We as a People

1. Staple Singers, "If You're Ready (Come Go with Me)," by Homer Banks, Carl Hampton, and Raymond Jackson, track 2 on *Be What You Are*, Stax, 1973.

2. Martin Luther King Jr., "I've Been to the Mountaintop," speech on April 3, 1968, at Bishop Charles Mason Temple, Memphis, Tennessee, accessed via Martin Luther King, Jr., Research and Education Institute, Stanford University, https://kinginstitute.stanford.edu/encyclopedia/ive-been -mountaintop?wpmm=1&wpisrc=nl_daily202.

3. Eddie S. Glaude Jr., *Exodus!: Religion, Race, and Nation in Early Nineteenth-Century Black America* (Chicago: University of Chicago Press, 2000).

4. Albert J. Raboteau, *A Fire in the Bones: Reflections on African-American Religious History* (Boston: Beacon Press, 1995).

5. Michael C. Dawson, *Black Visions: The Roots of Contemporary African-American Political Ideologies* (Chicago: University of Chicago Press, 2001); Melanye T. Price, *Dreaming Blackness: Black Nationalism and African American Public Opinion* (New York: New York University Press, 2009).

6. Tommy Shelby, *We Who Are Dark: The Philosophical Foundations of Black Solidarity* (Cambridge, MA: Belknap Press, 2005).

7. Eugene Robinson, *Disintegration: The Splintering of Black America* (New York: Anchor, 2011).

8. Ralph Waldo Emerson, "Self-Reliance," in *Essays, First Series*, 1841, https://archive.vcu.edu/english/engweb/transcendentalism/authors /emerson/essays/selfreliance.html.

9. Toni Morrison, *The Origins of Others* (Cambridge, MA: Harvard University Press, 2017).

10. Martin Luther King Jr., "Unfulfilled Hopes," sermon on April 5, 1959, at Dexter Avenue Baptist Church, accessed via Martin Luther King, Jr., Research and Education Institute, Stanford University, https://kinginstitute .stanford.edu/king-papers/documents/unfulfilled-hopes-0.

11. Robert Johnson, "Hellhound on My Trail," Vocalion, 1937. There are a variety of interpretation of this song: Robert Palmer, *Deep Blues* (New

York: Viking Press, 1981); Elijah Wald, *Escaping the Delta: Robert Johnson and the Invention of the Blues* (New York: Harper Collins, 2004); Karlos K. Hill, "The Lynching Blues: Robert Johnson's 'Hellhound on My Trail' as a Lynching Ballad," *Study the South*, Center for the Study of Southern Culture at the University of Mississippi, May 11, 2015, https://southernstudies.olemiss.edu/study-the-south/the-lynching-blues. Johnson left his lyrics open enough for the interpreter to find their own meaning. What is certain is the singer is haunted by impending death, no matter the background source to his lyrics.

12. Martin Luther King Jr., "The Montgomery Bus Boycott," speech on December 5, 1955, at Holt Street Baptist Church, accessed via Black Past, http://www.blackpast.org/1955-martin-luther-king-jr-montgomery-bus-boycott.

13. Michael Eric Dyson, *I May Not Get There with You: The True Martin Luther King, Jr.* (New York: Free Press, 2000).

14. W. E. B. Du Bois, *The Souls of Black Folk*, eds. David W. Blight and Robert Gooding-Williams (Boston: Bedford, 1997).

15. Edwidge Danticat, *Create Dangerously: The Immigrant Artist at Work* (New York: Vintage Books, 2011).

16. Martin Luther King Jr., "I've Been to the Mountaintop," speech on April 3, 1968, at Bishop Charles Mason Temple, Memphis, Tennessee, accessed via Martin Luther King, Jr., Research and Education Institute, Stanford University, https://kinginstitute.stanford.edu/encyclopedia/ive-been-mountaintop?wpmm=1&wpisrc=nl_daily202.

17. Duke Ellington, "Come Sunday," Mahalia Jackson, vocalist, track 4 on *Black, Brown, and Beige Suite*, Columbia Records, 1958.

8. The World House

1. "He's Got the Whole World in His Hands," track 14 on *Mahalia Jackson Sings America's Favorite Hymns*, CBS, 1971.

2. Martin Luther King Jr., "Acceptance Speech," December 10, 1964, Nobel Peace Prize in Oslo, https://www.nobelprize.org/prizes/peace/1964/king/26142-martin-luther-king-jr-acceptance-speech-1964/.

3. Martin Luther King Jr., *Why We Can't Wait* (New York: Harper & Row, 1964).

4. Martin Luther King Jr., *Where Do We Go from Here: Chaos or Community?* (Boston: Beacon Press, 1967), 179.

5. Cedric J. Robinson, *Black Marxism: The Making of Radical Tradition*, 3rd ed. (Chapel Hill: University of North Carolina Press, 1983).

6. Michael A. Gomez, *Exchanging Our Country Marks: The Transformation of African Identities in the Colonial and Antebellum South* (Chapel Hill: University of North Carolina Press, 1998).

7. W. E. B. Du Bois, *The Souls of Black Folk*, eds. David W. Blight and Robert Gooding-Williams (Boston: Bedford, 1997).

8. Barbara J. Fields, "'Origins of the New South' and the Negro Question," *Journal of Southern History* 67, no. 4 (November 2001).

9. Karl Marx and Friedrich Engels, *Karl Marx and Friedrich Engels, Selected Works*, vol. 1 (Moscow: Progress Publishers, 1969), 98–137.

10. Du Bois, *The Souls of Black Folk*, 13.

11. Woodrow Wilson, "Making the World 'Safe for Democracy': Woodrow Wilson Asks for War," address to Congress on April 2, 1917, History Matters, http://historymatters.gmu.edu/d/4943/.

12. Cornel West, *The Ethical Dimension of Marxist Thought* (New York: New York University Press, 1991).

13. Martin Luther King Jr., "Three Essays on Religion," in *The Papers of Martin Luther King, Jr.*, eds. Clayborne Carson et al., vol. 6, *Advocate of the Social Gospel, September 1948–March 1963* (Berkeley, CA: University of California Press, 2007).

14. Kevin M. Kruse, *One Nation Under God: How Corporate America Invented Christian America* (New York: Basic Books, 2015).

15. Andrew Glass, "Bernard Baruch Coins Term 'Cold War,' April 16, 1947," *Politico*, April 16, 2010, https://www.politico.com/story/2010/04/bernard-baruch-coins-term-cold-war-april-16-1947-035862.

16. Kevin K. Gaines, *American Africans in Ghana: Black Expatriates and the Civil Rights Era* (Chapel Hill: University of North Carolina Press, 2008); Martin Luther King Jr., "The Birth of a New Age," speech on August 11, 1956, at Alpha Phi Alpha, Buffalo, New York, accessed via Martin Luther King, Jr., Research and Education Institute, Stanford University, https://kinginstitute.stanford.edu/king-papers/documents/birth-new-age-address-delivered-11-august-1956-fiftieth-anniversary-alpha-phi.

17. Langston Hughes, "200 Years of Afro-American Poetry," accessed via the Poetry Foundation, https://www.poetryfoundation.org/articles/69396 /200-years-of-afro-american-poetry.

18. Franklin D. Roosevelt, "Four Freedoms," Annual Message to Congress, January 6, 1941, Records of the United States Senate, SEN 77A-H1, Record Group 46, National Archives.

19. Martin Luther King Jr., "The Birth of a New Age," speech on August 11, 1956, at Alpha Phi Alpha, Buffalo, New York, accessed via Martin Luther King, Jr., Research and Education Institute, Stanford University, https://kinginstitute.stanford.edu/king-papers/documents/birth-new-age -address-delivered-11-august-1956-fiftieth-anniversary-alpha-phi.

20. King, *Where Do We Go*, 180.

21. John Dewey, *A Common Faith* (New Haven, CT: Yale University Press, 2013).

22. King, *Where Do We Go*, 179.

23. King, 201–202.

9. All Labor Has Dignity

1. Nina Simone, "Work Song," by Nat Adderley and Oscar Brown Jr., track 6 on *Forbidden Fruit*, Coplix, 1961.

2. Martin Luther King Jr., *"All Labor Has Dignity,"* ed. Michael K. Honey (Boston: Beacon Press, 2011).

3. King, *"All Labor Has Dignity."*

4. Orlando Patterson, *Slavery and Social Death: A Comparative Study* (Cambridge, MA: Harvard University Press, 1982).

5. Maria W. Stewart, "Why Sit Ye Here and Die?" speech on September 31, 1832, at Franklin Hall, accessed via Black Past, http://www.blackpast .org/1832-maria-w-stewart-why-sit-ye-here-and-die.

6. Henry Highland Garnet, "An Address to the Slaves of the United States," The National Negro Convention, Buffalo, New York, 1843, in *Crossing the Danger Water: Three Hundred Years of African-American Writing*, ed. Deirdre Mullane (New York: Doubleday, 1993).

7. Douglas A. Blackmon, *Slavery by Another Name: The Re-enslavement of Black Americans from the Civil War to World War II* (New York: Anchor, 2009); Talitha L. LeFlouria, *Chained in Silence: Black Women and Convict Labor in the New South* (University of North Carolina Press, 2016).

8. Mary McLeod Bethune, "What Does American Democracy Mean to Me?" speech on November 23, 1939, at America's Town Meeting of the Air, New York City, accessed via Say It Plain: A Century of Great African American Speeches, American Public Media, http://americanradioworks .publicradio.org/features/sayitplain/mmbethune.html.

9. Tera W. Hunter, *To 'Joy My Freedom: Southern Black Women's Lives and Labor After the Civil War* (Cambridge, MA: Harvard University Press,1997); Joe William Trotter Jr., *Workers on Arrival: Black Labor in the Making of America* (Berkley: University of California Press, 2019).

10. Ella Baker and Marvel Cooke, "The Slave Market," *Crisis* 42, November 1935, https://caringlabor.wordpress.com/2010/11/24/ella-baker-and-marvel -cooke-the-slave-market/.

11. Claudia Jones, "An End to the Neglect of the Problems of the Negro Woman!" in *Words of Fire: An Anthology of African-American Feminist Thought,* ed. Beverly Guy-Sheftall (New York: The New Press, 1995), 109–110.

12. Jones, "Problems of the Negro Woman,"109.

13. Ann Petry, *The Street* (New York: Houghton Mifflin Company, 1946).

14. Josh Levin, "The Welfare Queen," *Slate*, December 19, 2013, http://www .slate.com/articles/news_and_politics/history/2013/12/linda_taylor _welfare_queen_ronald_reagan_made_her_a_notorious_american _villain.html; Gene Demby, "The Truth Behind the Lies of the Original 'Welfare Queen,'" *Code Switch*, NPR, December 20, 2013, https://www .npr.org/sections/codeswitch/2013/12/20/255819681/the-truth-behind -the-lies-of-the-original-welfare-queen; Dahleen Glanton, "The Myth of the 'Welfare Queen' Endures, and Children Pay the Price," *Chicago Tribune,* May 17, 2018, http://www.chicagotribune.com/news/columnists /glanton/ct-met-dahleen-glanton-welfare-queen-20180516-story .html; Mindy Thompson Fullilove, E. Anne Lown, and Robert E. Ful- lilove, "Crack 'Hos and Skeezers: Traumatic Experiences of Women Crack Users," *The Journal of Sex Research* 29, no. 2 (May 1992): 275–87, accessed September 23, 2020, http://www.jstor.org/stable/3812633.

15. Deborah Gray White, *Ar'n't I a Woman?: Female Slaves in the Plantation South* (New York: W. W. Norton & Company, 1999).

16. Steve Estes, *I Am a Man!: Race, Manhood, and the Civil Rights Movement* (Chapel Hill: University of North Carolina Press, 2005).

17. Martin Luther King Jr., Speech to the UAW 25th Anniversary Dinner, April 27, 1961, accessed via UAW-GM Talks, https://uawgmtalks.word press.com/2015/12/17/the-reverend-martin-luther-king-jr-speech-to -the-uaw-25th-anniversary-dinner-april-27-1961/.

18. Premilla Nadsen, *Welfare Warriors: The Welfare Rights Movement in the United States* (New York: Routledge, 2005); Felicia Kornbluh, *The Battle for Welfare Rights: Politics and Poverty in Modern America* (Philadelphia: University of Pennsylvania Press, 2007); Frances Fox Piven and Richard A. Cloward, *Regulating the Poor: The Function of Public Welfare*, rev. ed. (New York: Vintage, 1993); *America's War on Poverty*, episode 5, "My Brother's Keeper," directed by Leslie D. Farrell, PBS Documentary Series, 1995.

19. David Holley, "Mechanical Cotton Picker," EH.net, Economic History Association, https://eh.net/encyclopedia/mechanical-cotton-picker/.

20. Daniel Patrick Moynihan, *The Negro Family: The Case for National Action*, Office of Policy Planning and Research, United States Department of Labor, March 1965, https://www.dol.gov/general/aboutdol/history/webid -moynihan.

21. Martin Luther King Jr., chap. 28 in *The Autobiography of Martin Luther King, Jr.*, ed. Clayborne Carson (New York: Grand Central Publishing, 2001), https://kinginstitute.stanford.edu/king-papers/publications/autobio graphy-martin-luther-king-jr-contents/chapter-28-chicago-campaign.

22. Martin Luther King Jr., *Where Do We Go from Here: Chaos or Community?* (Boston: Beacon Press, 1967), 149.

10. Growing Up King

1. Isley Brothers, "Fight the Power," track 1 on *The Heat Is On*, Epic and T-Neck, 1975.

2. Dexter Scott King and Ralph Wiley, *Growing Up King: An Intimate Memoir* (New York: Grand Central Publishing, 2003).

3. *To Sleep with Anger*, directed by Charles Burnett (1990; Criterion Collection, 2019), https://www.criterion.com/films/29567-to-sleep-with-anger.

4. Martin Luther King Jr., "I Have a Dream," speech on August 28, 1963, at the March on Washington for Jobs and Freedom, accessed via Martin Luther King, Jr., Research and Education Institute, Stanford University,

https://kinginstitute.stanford.edu/king-papers/documents/i-have
-dream-address-delivered-march-washington-jobs-and-freedom.

5. Mary Pattillo, *Black Picket Fences: Privilege and Peril Among the Black Middle Class*, 2nd ed. (Chicago: University of Chicago Press, 2013).

6. Martin Luther, *Commentary on the Sermon on the Mount*, trans. Charles A. Hay (Philadelphia: Lutheran Publication Society, 1892), 236, https://babel.hathitrust.org/cgi/pt?id=nnc1.cr60048620&view=1up&seq=240.

7. Wilson Jeremiah Moses, *Afrotopia: The Roots of African American Popular History* (Cambridge: Cambridge University Press, 1998).

8. Gene Demby with Ezra Edelman, "I'm Not Back I'm O.J." *Code Switch*, NPR, October 12, 2016, https://www.npr.org/2016/10/12/497565530/encore-im-not-black-im-o-j.

9. Jelani Cobb, ed., *The Essential Kerner Commission Report* (New York: Liveright Publishing, 2021).

10. David L. Chappell, *Waking from the Dream: The Struggle for Civil Rights in the Shadow of Martin Luther King Jr.* (New York: Random House, 2014).

11. Robert L. Heilbroner, "The Gloomy Presentiments of Parson Malthus and David Ricardo," in *The Worldly Philosophers: The Lives, Times, and Ideas of the Great Economic Thinkers*, 7th ed. (New York: Touchstone, 1999).

12. James Forman Jr., "How Black Leaders Unwittingly Contributed to the Era of Mass Incarceration," interview by Terry Gross, *Fresh Air*, NPR, May 11, 2018, https://www.npr.org/2018/05/11/610385205/how-black-leaders-unwittingly-contributed-to-the-era-of-mass-incarceration.

13. Shelby Steele, *The Content of Our Character: A New Vision of Race in America* (New York: Harper Perennial, 1998).

14. Martin Luther King Jr., "The Man Who Was a Fool," sermon on March 6, 1961, at the Detroit Council of Churches' Noon Lenten Services, accessed via Martin Luther King, Jr., Research and Education Institute, Stanford University, https://kinginstitute.stanford.edu/king-papers/documents/man-who-was-fool-sermon-delivered-detroit-council-churches-noon-lenten.

15. "Muhammad Ali—The Measure of a Man," *Freedomways* 7, no. 2 (Spring 1967): 101–102, https://www.aavw.org/protest/homepage_ali.html.

16. "War of Words Between LeBron James and Laura Ingraham," ABC News, February 18, 2018, https://youtu.be/RNLl2C1Pn-I.

17. James Weldon Johnson, "Lift Every Voice and Sing," 1900, https://www.poetryfoundation.org/poems/46549/lift-every-voice-and-sing. For a history of the song, see Imani Perry, *May We Forever Stand: A History of the Black National Anthem* (Chapel Hill: University of North Carolina Press, 2018).

18. "African American Students in Higher Education," Factsheets: African-American Students, Postsecondary National Policy Institute, June 12, 2020, https://pnpi.org/african-american-students/.

19. Stephen L. Carter, *Reflections of an Affirmative Action Baby* (New York: Basic Books, 1991).

20. William Julius Wilson, *The Declining Significance of Race: Blacks and Changing American Institutions* (Chicago: University of Chicago, 1978).

21. Tom Wolfe, "The 'Me' Decade and the Third Great Awakening," *New York Magazine*, August 23, 1976.

22. Jay-Z, "The Story of O.J.," by Shawn Carter, Dion Wilson, Nina Simone, Gene Redd, Jimmy Crosby, track 2 on *4:44*, Roc Nation, 2017.

23. Adam Serwer, "Bill Cosby's Famous 'Pound Cake' Speech, Annotated," BuzzFeed News, July 9, 2015, https://www.buzzfeednews.com/article/adamserwer/bill-cosby-pound-for-pound; Michael Eric Dyson, *Is Bill Cosby Right? Or Has the Black Middle Class Lost Its Mind?* (New York: Basic Books, 2005); "Bill Cosby Famous Pound Cake Speech," posted by Mnangagwa, May 9, 2009, https://www.youtube.com/watch?v=_Gh3_e3mDQ8.

24. W. E. B. Du Bois, "On Being Ashamed of Oneself: An Essay on Race Pride," *Crisis* 40, no. 9 (New York: Crisis Publishing, 1933).

25. Orlando Patterson, *Freedom*, vol. 1, *Freedom in the Making of Western Culture* (New York: Basic Books, 1991).

26. Martin Luther King Jr., "Facing the Challenge of a New Age," speech on January 1, 1957, at the NAACP Emancipation Rally in Atlanta, Georgia, accessed via Martin Luther King, Jr., Research and Education Institute, Stanford University, https://kinginstitute.stanford.edu/king-papers/documents/facing-challenge-new-age-address-delivered-naacp-emancipation-day-rally.

27. Dean Lawrence Carter, quoted in "A Nation Remembers the Grace and Strength of Coretta Scott King 1927–2006," by Andrew Young, *Ebony*, April 2006, 192.

28. Martin Luther King Jr., "Coretta," in *The Autobiography of Martin Luther King, Jr.*, ed. Clayborne Carson (New York: Grand Central Publishing, 2001), https://kinginstitute.stanford.edu/king-papers/publications/autobiography -martin-luther-king-jr-contents/chapter-5-coretta.

29. Aicha FD, "Lupe Fiasco Quits Twitter," *XXL*, January 14, 2015, https:// www.xxlmag.com/lupe-fiasco-quits-twitter-says-never-really-liked -dealing-public/.

30. Peter Kihss, "'Benign Neglect' on Race Is Proposed by Moynihan," *New York Times*, March 1, 1970, https://www.nytimes.com/1970/03/01/archives /benign-neglect-on-race-is-proposed-by-moynihan-moynihan-urges.html.

31. "Once to Every Man and Nation," James Russell Lowell, 1845, https:// hymnary.org/text/once_to_every_man_and_nation.

32. Martin Luther King Jr., "The Drum Major Instinct," speech on February 4, 1968, at Ebenezer Baptist Church, accessed via Martin Luther King, Jr., Research and Education Institute, Stanford University, https:// kinginstitute.stanford.edu/king-papers/documents/drum-major -instinct-sermon-delivered-ebenezer-baptist-church.

11. The Content of Our Character

1. Billie Holiday and Arthur Herzog Jr., "Don't Explain," track 3 on *The Lady Sings*, Decca, 1956.

2. Anastasia C. Curwood, *Stormy Weather: Middle-Class African American Marriages Between the Two World Wars* (Chapel Hill: University of North Carolina Press, 2010).

3. Sigmund Freud, *Civilization and Its Discontents* (New York: W. W. Norton, 2010); Herbert Marcuse, *Eros and Civilization: A Philosophical Inquiry into Freud* (Boston, MA: Beacon Press, 1974).

4. James Cone, *Martin and Malcolm and America: A Dream or a Nightmare* (Maryknoll, NY: Orbis Books, 2012).

5. Keeanga-Yamahatta Taylor, ed., *How We Get Free: Black Feminism and the Combahee River Collective* (Chicago: Haymarket Books, 2017).

6. Édouard Glissant, *Poetics of Relation*, trans. Betsy Wing (Ann Arbor: University of Michigan Press, 1997).

7. Hannah Arendt, *On Violence* (New York: Harcourt, 1970).

8. Martin Luther King Jr., "Our God Is Marching On," speech on March 25, 1965, Montgomery, Alabama, accessed via Martin Luther King, Jr.,

Research and Education Institute, Stanford University, https://king institute.stanford.edu/our-god-marching.

9. "Sex Tapes, FBI Smears and the Double Life of an All Too Human Saint: The Other Side to the Martin Luther King Story," *The Daily Mail*, August 30, 2013, https://www.dailymail.co.uk/news/article-2407403/Sex-tapes -FBI-smears-double-life-human-saint-The-Martin-Luther-King-story.html.

10. Martin Luther King Sr., *Daddy King: An Autobiography* (New York: William Morrow, 1980).

11. "From the Archive, 1 July 1974: Martin Luther King's Mother Slain in Church," *Guardian*, July 1, 2014, https://www.theguardian.com/world /2014/jul/01/martin-luther-kings-mother-slain-in-church-1974.

12. Rayford W. Logan, *The Betrayal of the Negro: From Rutherford B. Hayes to Woodrow Wilson* (New York: Da Capo Press, 1997).

13. Jeff Bridgers, "Du Bois's American Negro Exhibit for the 1900 Paris Exposition," *Picture This* (blog), Library of Congress, February 28, 2014, https://blogs.loc.gov/picturethis/2014/02/du-boiss-american-negro -exhibit-for-the-1900-paris-exposition/; Annette Gordon-Reed, "The Color Line," *New York Review*, August 19, 2021, https://www.nybooks.com /articles/2021/08/19/du-bois-color-line-paris-exposition/.

14. Allison Dorsey, *To Build Our Lives Together: Community Formation in Black Atlanta, 1875–1906* (Athens, GA: University of Georgia Press, 2004).

15. Willie Christine King Farris, "Young Martin: From Childhood Through College," *Ebony* 41, no. 3 (January 1986): 56–58.

16. Martin Luther King Jr., "To Alberta Williams King," October 1–31, 1948, accessed via Martin Luther King, Jr., Research and Education Institute, Stanford University, https://kinginstitute.stanford.edu/king-papers /documents/alberta-williams-king-4.

17. Martin Luther King Jr., "The Vision of the World Made New," speech on September 9, 1954, to the Women's Convention Auxiliary, National Baptist Convention, accessed via Martin Luther King, Jr., Research and Education Institute, Stanford University, https://kinginstitute.stanford .edu/encyclopedia/king-delivers-vision-world-made-new-womens -convention-auxiliary-national-baptist.

18. Evelyn Brooks Higginbotham, *Righteous Discontent: The Women's Movement in the Black Baptist Church, 1880–1920* (Cambridge, MA: Harvard University Press, 1994).

19. Christine King Farris, *Through It All: Reflections on My Life, My Family, and My Faith* (New York: Atria Books, 2009).

20. Danielle L. McGuire, *At the Dark End of the Street: Black Women, Rape, and Resistance—A New History of the Civil Rights Movement from Rosa Parks to the Rise of Black Power* (New York: Vintage Books, 2011).

21. See letters between the Kings in the Martin Luther King Jr. Collection, Morehouse College, https://www.morehouse.edu/life/campus/martin-luther-king-jr-collection/.

22. Ralph David Abernathy, *And the Walls Came Tumbling Down* (New York: Harper and Row, 1989).

23. Taylor, *How We Get Free.*

24. Higginbotham, *Righteous Discontent.*

25. Bettye Collier-Thomas, *Jesus, Jobs, and Justice: African American Women and Religion* (New York: Knopf, 2010).

26. Pauli Murray, "Jim Crow and Jane Crow," in *Black Women in White America: A Documentary History,* ed. Gerda Lerner (New York: Vintage, 1992), 592–598.

12. A Stone of Hope

1. Ben Harper, "How Many Miles Must We March," track 11 on *Welcome to the Cruel World*, Virgin, 1994.

2. Robert Hayden, "Frederick Douglass," in *Collected Poems of Robert Hayden,* ed. Frederick Glaysher (New York: W. W. Norton, 1966), accessed via The Poetry Foundation, https://www.poetryfoundation.org/poems/46460/frederick-douglass.

3. Howard Thurman, *Jesus and the Disinherited* (Boston: Beacon Press, 1996).

4. Orlando Patterson, *Slavery and Social Death: A Comparative Study* (Cambridge, MA: Harvard University Press, 1982).

5. "I'm on My Way to Canaan," Mahalia Jackson, track 6 on *The Apollo Sessions, Vol. 2,* Apollo, 1995.

6. Langston Hughes, "Dream of Freedom," in *The Collected Poems of Langston Hughes,* eds. Arnold Rampersad and David Roessel (New York: Vintage Classic, 1994), 542.

7. Mohandas Gandhi, "Essence of Democracy," The Mind of Mahatma Gandhi, Gandhian Institutions: Bombay Sarvodaya Mandal and Gandhi

Research Foundation, https://www.mkgandhi.org/momgandhi/chap72.htm.

8. Kendrick Lamar Duckworth and Abel Tesfaye, "Pray for Me," by Duckworth, Tesfaye, Adam King Feeney, and Martin McKinney, track 14 on *Black Panther*, Top Dawg, Aftermath, and Interscope, 2018.

9. Martin Luther King Jr., "Address at Public Meeting of the Southern Christian Ministers Conference of Mississippi," September 23, 1959, accessed via Martin Luther King, Jr., Research and Education Institute, Stanford University, https://kinginstitute.stanford.edu/king-papers/documents/address-public-meeting-southern-christian-ministers-conference-mississippi.

10. Barack Obama, *The Audacity of Hope: Thoughts of Reclaiming the American Dream* (New York: Crown Publishers, 2006).

11. "Heav'n, Heav'n," Marian Anderson, vocalist, by Harry T. Burleigh, track 16 on *He's Got the Whole World in His Hands: Spirituals*, RCA Victor, 1965.

12. Howard Thurman, *With Head and Heart: The Autobiography of Howard Thurman* (New York: Harcourt Brace Jovanovich, 1979), 20–21.

13. Thurman, *With Head and Heart*, 21.

14. W. E. B. Du Bois, *The Souls of Black Folk*, eds. David W. Blight and Robert Gooding-Williams (Boston: Bedford, 1997).

15. Randal Jelks, "'Of Our Spiritual Strivings': Faith, Justice, and the Teaching of the Humanities," Third Annual Conversation on the Liberal Arts, Gaede Institute for the Liberal Arts, Westmont College, January 31–February 1, 2003, https://classic.westmont.edu/institute/conversations/2003_program/papers.

16. Martin Luther King Jr., "Draft of Chapter X, 'Shattered Dreams,'" sermon on April 5, 1959, at Dexter Avenue Baptist Church, accessed via Martin Luther King, Jr., Research and Education Institute, Stanford University, https://kinginstitute.stanford.edu/king-papers/documents/draft-chapter-x-shattered-dreams.

17. Martin Luther King Jr., "MIA Mass Meeting at Holt Street Baptist Church," speech given on December 5, 1955, in Montgomery, Alabama, accessed via Martin Luther King, Jr., Research and Education Institute, Stanford University, https://kinginstitute.stanford.edu/king-papers/documents/mia-mass-meeting-holt-street-baptist-church.

18. Martin Luther King Jr., "I Have a Dream," speech on August 28, 1963, at the March on Washington for Jobs and Freedom, accessed via Martin Luther King, Jr., Research and Education Institute, Stanford University, https://kinginstitute.stanford.edu/king-papers/documents/i-have-dream-address-delivered-march-washington-jobs-and-freedom.

Epilogue

1. Marvin P. Gaye, "What's Going On," by Alfred W. Cleveland, Marvin P. Gaye, and Renaldo Benson, track 1 on *What's Going On*, Tamla, 1971.

2. Jürgen Habermas, *The Theory of Communicative Action*, vol. 1, *Reason and Rationalization of Society* (Cambridge, England: Polity Press, 1984).

3. Robert S. Ellwood, *The Fifties Spiritual Marketplace: American Religion in a Decade of Conflict* (New Brunswick, NJ: Rutgers University Press, 1997).

4. Martin Luther King Jr., "'Facing the Challenge of a New Age,' Address Delivered at the First Annual Institute on Nonviolence and Social Change," accessed via Martin Luther King, Jr., Research and Education Institute, Stanford University, https://kinginstitute.stanford.edu/king-papers/documents/facing-challenge-new-age-address-delivered-first-annual-institute-nonviolence.

5. Martin Luther King Jr., "Beyond Vietnam," April 4, 1967, speech at Riverside Church, New York City, accessed via Martin Luther King, Jr., Research and Education Institute, Stanford University, https://kinginstitute.stanford.edu/king-papers/documents/beyond-vietnam.